The Investor's
Self-Teaching Seminars

UNDERSTANDING AND
MANAGING INVESTMENT
RISK & RETURN

The Investor's
Self-Teaching Seminars

UNDERSTANDING AND MANAGING INVESTMENT
RISK & RETURN

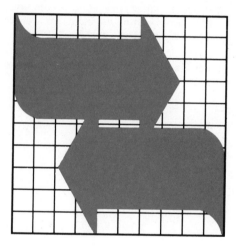

One of a Series of Hands-On Workshops
Dedicated to the Serious Investor

David L. Scott

PROBUS PUBLISHING COMPANY
Chicago, Illinois

Library of Congress Cataloging-in-Publication Data Available

ISBN 1-55738-105-4

Printed in the United States of America

1   2   3   4   5   6   7   8   9   0

CONTENTS

FOREWORD

The lengthy bull market in common stocks that commenced in August 1982 caused investors to tuck risk into the far recesses of their minds. Then came October 19, 1987's, "Meltdown Monday" with its dramatic decline and a near calamity in the financial markets. Actually, for some individuals it was more than just a near calamity. The sudden and generally unexpected free-fall of stock prices brought investors back to earth with such a thud that many of them still have not recovered.

Risks are always with us, and it is important that investors consider these risks as part of their financial planning. Before planning can take place, however, it is first necessary to understand what these risks are and how they apply to the ever-increasing variety of investments being made available to investors. Never before has there been such a great abundance of investment alternatives. Only by understanding the risks applicable to these alternatives can an investor effectively control the risks while building a portfolio.

Different individuals are in different financial situations with disparate wants and needs. This great diversity in the status of individual investors brings with it a varying ability to absorb risks. Some individuals may have significantly more to fear from inflation than from changing interest rates or market fluctuations, for example. Because of the varying ability to absorb risks, it is crucial that the investor understand which risks are most important and what types of investments can provide the greatest degree of protection from those risks.

This book attempts to present the concept of investment risk in a manner that can be understood by the average investor. The various uncertainties that face individual investors are discussed in a nontechnical and nonthreatening manner with the goal of allowing readers to put the ideas to use in building their own investment portfolios.

The book first presents a general concept of risk: what it is and how it affects virtually all investments. The following two chapters discuss the various risks that cause uncertain rates of return among investments; unexpected inflation, uncertain interest rates, uncertain business conditions, excessive borrowing, unpredictable market cycles, and potential difficulty in disposing of an asset. The discussion of individual risks is followed by chapters on individual investment categories and the risks that cause the greatest uncertainties to owners of these assets. The final chapter is devoted to a discussion of how an individual investor can put together an investment portfolio that best minimizes the important risks that have been identified by the investor.

In many instances common sense will go a long way in controlling risk. When someone promises an unrealistically high return, there is every reason to suspect that the return truly is unrealistic. At least, it is unrealistic to think that such a high return can occur without substantial risk. Because the investment world is so competitive, it is generally possible to earn substantially higher returns only by incurring greater risks.

Investors most often lose substantial amounts of money when they get overly greedy. Individuals read in magazines how other investors have become wealthy, or they hear their friends brag on how much they have made on such and such an investment. The tendency is to take the plunge in seeking riches that will provide material for new stories. Unfortunately, the likely result is something even the family dog won't want to hear.

Nothing is wrong with undertaking risky investments so long as the investor understands the possible consequences. Financial theory tells us that risky investments have higher expected returns. It is just that the higher the expected return becomes, the less certain the investor is to actually earn such a return. This, of course, is the risk.

An investor's tolerance for risk is more than just a pencil and paper analysis of the pros and cons of the uncertainties surrounding an individual investment or portfolio of investments. Without question, many investors are so indisposed to risk that a little of it goes a long way, no matter what the investor's age, financial status, or goals. An investment advisor may examine the financial status of an individual investor and decide that it would be prudent to pursue a more risky investment path in search of additional return. On paper this conclusion may well be justified. However, if the individual investor is so afraid of potential losses that substantial worry would result, then the potential for additional return is likely outweighed by peace of mind. There are more important things in life than eking out an extra quarter of a percent.

I would like to thank a number of people and organizations that contributed to the completion of this book. First, I express appreciation to my wife, Kay, for allowing me to spend hours, days, and weekends in front of my trusty AT&T computer. Now that this manuscript is complete, we may eat fewer nacho chips, tacos, and pizzas. Also, I appreciate the fact that our dean, Ken Stanley, supports these activities and had the foresight to equip the business faculty at Valdosta State with superb computer facilities. My good and computer-literate friend, Steve Parrish, was kind enough to produce the graphs in his small abode behind the local K Mart. Also, thanks to student assistant Bart Holt for his help in tracking down data for the graphs and tables. Finally, thanks to the Graduate Research Advisory Committee at Valdosta State College, which provided partial funding to assist with the incidental expenses involved in producing the manuscript.

David L. Scott
Valdosta, Georgia

Chapter
One

UNDERSTANDING INVESTMENT RISK

There is no denying that individuals live in an environment that is full of risks. Risks of varying degrees of seriousness are always lurking nearby: the possibility of an accident while driving an automobile; of suddenly contracting a serious disease; of having a home damaged by fire or violent weather; of falling in the shower; of purchasing a faulty computer from a mail-order firm that soon goes out of business, and so on. The compendium of risks encountered in everyday life seems to be endless.

Although the variety of risks inherent in investing is certainly less diverse and less physically painful than some of the pitfalls just noted, experienced investors have nonetheless learned that numerous risks are indigenous to nearly all investment vehicles. Investors may see their investment in a business disappear because of a lack of customers during a period of economic recession. They may find that dividends or interest income from security holdings are reduced or eliminated because the payor is no longer financially able to make payments. They may discover that inflation has eaten away at the real value of their investment such that the returns are puny or even negative when adjusted for changes in the cost things they must buy.

There are many reasons that an investment may produce unexpected results. Among even the best-known and most frequently used investments are often serious risks that tend to remain hidden. So, if risk is everywhere, why is it not always clearly evident? Why are investors frequently surprised when favorable expectations turn into major disappointments? Before these questions can be addressed, risk must first be identified. If risk cannot be recognized, it certainly cannot be controlled.

WHAT IS INVESTMENT RISK?

As a general concept, investment risk refers to an uncertain rate of return. For a single investment or group of investments, the less certain the rate of return, the greater the risk of ownership. Viewed from the opposite perspective, the greater the certainty of an investment's rate of return, the less the risk of owning the investment. If there is absolutely no question about the rate of return that an investment will provide, then there is no risk to owning that investment. Unfortunately, these no-risk gems are few and, when they are located, tend to offer relatively meager returns.

An investment's rate of return may be uncertain for any number of reasons. For example, there is always the possibility that a company's directors will reduce the dividend on its common stock or that a municipality will be unable to make the interest payments on its bonds. Likewise, a period of rapid price inflation will significantly reduce the real value of a bond's principal. As if inflation is not ominous enough, rising interest rates that frequently accompany inflation will exert downward pressure on the prices of outstanding bonds.

In addition to uncertain income sources such as dividends or rent payments, uncertainty can also stem from doubt about the money an investment will fetch if it is sold. For example, a high-grade, long-term bond produces semi-annual interest payments that are reasonably certain to occur on the scheduled dates. Even if the bond is of the very highest grade, however, there is no way of knowing for certain how much the security will bring if it must be sold prior to maturity. Also, there is no way to determine how much of the bond's interest and principal will be eaten away by inflation during the years that the bond is owned.

The world of available investments is quite diverse, so that risks vary considerably among investment alternatives. Some investments, such as real estate and new issues of common stocks, tend to subject their owners to a great amount of risk. At the same time, other investments, such as U.S. Treasury bills and short-term certificates of deposit, have very little uncertainty as to their rates of return. It is this certainty of return that is the paramount reason why individuals and institutions acquire these investments. Most people purchase certificates of deposit because they know exactly the amount of money they will receive and the precise date on which they will receive it.

The concept of investment risk can be illustrated with a numerical example. Suppose an investor is faced with two investment alternatives. Each investment requires an identical outlay of cash and each provides an expected return of 15 percent during its projected life of one year. The only difference between the two investments is that, while the annual rate of return on Investment A is a certain 15 percent, Investment B offers two possible outcomes, a return of 5 percent or a return of 25 percent. Each of these two returns on Investment B is equally likely, and there are no other possible outcomes. Thus, for Investment B, there is a 50 percent likelihood that the annual rate of return will be 5 percent and a 50 percent likelihood that the rate of return will be 25 percent. Investment B has the same expected rate of return as Investment A, even though there is no way to determine in advance whether the return on B will be 5 percent or 25 percent. A comparison of the possible outcomes and respective probabilities for each of the two investments is displayed in Exhibit 1–1.

A general formula for calculating an investment's expected rate of return is:

$$R = p_1 r_1 + p_2 r_2 + p_3 r_3 + \ldots + p_n r_n$$

where:

R = the investment's expected rate of return.

r = each possible rate of return that may actually occur.

p = the probability that a particular rate of return may occur. The sum of these probabilities must equal 100 percent.

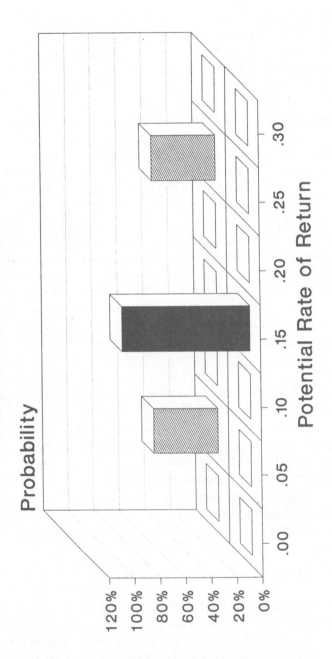

Figure 1–1
Potential Returns on Two Investments

1, 2, 3, . . . , n = the events. The first possible event is labeled "1", the second event "2", and so forth.

In the case of the two investment alternatives discussed above, the expected rate of return for Investment B would be calculated as:

$R_b =$ $p_1r_1 + p_2r_2$
$R_b =$ $(.50)(5\%) + (.50)(25\%)$
    $= (2.5\%) + (12.5\%) = 15\%.$

The expected rate of return for Investment A, which has only a single possible outcome, is calculated as:

$R_a =$ $(1.00)(15\%) = 15\%.$

This example demonstrates a central concept in the under-standing of investment risk. That is, the expected return and the return that actually occurs are frequently different. Several invest-ments can have exactly the same expected rate of return and yet produce substantially disparate results. An investment will always yield its expected rate of return only if no other outcome is pos-sible—in other words, if there is no risk. Having an investment that yields its expected rate of return is more the exception than the rule.

The more divergent an investment's potential returns the more risky the investment tends to be, because there is less certainty about what rate of return will actually result. Suppose, for example, that a third alternative, Investment C, has potential returns of nega-tive 15 percent and positive 45 percent, both of which are each equally likely. The expected return for Investment C will still be 15 percent (-15 percent times .5 plus 45 percent times .5), but the in-vestment is riskier than even Investment B, because Investment C's possible outcomes are more divergent.

The discussion has so far been limited to the risk and return on a single investment. This simplifies the analysis of risk and is a neces-sary first step in understanding what risk is and how to deal with it. What it leaves out, however, is how the addition or deletion of a particular investment affects an investor's total portfolio. The dis-tinction is important because it is the risk of all investments taken together that must be evaluated. This overall risk, or as it is more properly called, portfolio risk, will be discussed in more detail later.

HOW INVESTORS VIEW RISK

Investment theory assumes that investors prefer to know in advance the outcome of their investment decisions. In other words, investors like to be able to count on the exact amount of income that the investment of their hard-earned (or inherited) dollars will bring. With respect to the investment alternatives discussed above, a typical investor would prefer Investment A (the certain 15 percent return) to Investment B (the possibility of either a 5 percent or a 25 percent rate of return). Either of these alternatives would be preferable to the third hypothetical investment that provides the two potential returns of either negative 15 percent or positive 45 percent.

Although the majority of investors shy away from risk, there are exceptions to the rule. Without exceptions there would be no Las Vegas, no Kentucky Derby, and no state lotteries. Some individuals actively search for investments with a high degree of risk. These persons may willingly choose Investments B or C over Investment A, just as they may bet a longshot to win rather than the favorite to show. More excitement results from the possibility of making a lot or losing it all as compared to earning a modest return with more certainty.

Although exceptions exist, there is a conscious decision on the part of most investors to avoid risk unless they are properly compensated. Investors tend to pick the least risky investments in a world where investments offer the same expected return. But when expected returns vary, the selection process becomes considerably more complicated and requires that investors consider another variable.

If investors as a group tend to shun risk, then risky investments must offer higher expected yields in order to attract buyers. In the previous example, the majority of investors would be attracted to Investment A, as long as it offered exactly the same expected return as Investment B. If investors refuse to put their dollars into Investment B, then the expected rate of return must move above 15 percent if it is to attract potential investors.

As an investment's expected return increases, there will be some level at which investors will decide that the riskier investment is actually the preferred investment vehicle. A preference for the higher risk investment will not occur at the same expected return for all investors. Some investors can be coaxed into choosing a riskier investment without a large corresponding increase in the expected rate of return. Other, more conservative investors require a significant increase in incentive to accept an investment that may have only small additional risk. If there is a diversity of risk among investments, there is an equally diverse group of investors. It is these great differences in how individual investors view risk that permit the offering of such a great variety of investments.

The direct relationship between risk and return is at the core of investment theory. Low-risk investments tend to be accompanied by low expected returns, while high-risk investments are accompanied by high expected returns. This doesn't mean that an investor will be assured of earning the higher expected return of a high-risk investment. The actual return may be higher or considerably lower than the rate of return that is expected.

This old and established premise that investors must accept additional risk in order to obtain a higher expected return is a concept that is frequently overlooked by many investors. In reaching for greater returns, it is easy to rationalize that a particular investment is "special." Perhaps a broker presents a convincing argument that there is something unique about the investment. He may infer that other investors haven't yet found out about the investment or that everyone else has overlooked something crucial to its valuation. In all too many instances, however, investors simply want to be convinced. People tend to rationalize when they get greedy.

RISK BENCHMARKS

The risk-return relationship is forged on the basis of the rate of return available on risk-free investments. The risk-free rate is the minimum acceptable return that establishes the standard by which all other investments must be judged. The higher the risk-free rate of return, the higher the return that all investments must provide.

With the perceived strength of the United States government guarantee of repayment combined with a huge secondary market, short-term Treasury securities are generally considered to be riskless investments. Investors purchase U.S. Treasury securities in large part because they are absolutely certain that their money will be returned at maturity. In addition, investors are confident that, if they wish to sell the securities prior to maturity, there will be an active market and relatively small transaction fees. With short maturities there will be little price variation caused by changing market rates of interest.

At the opposite end of the risk spectrum are investments such as precious metals, undeveloped real estate, futures contracts, and speculative common stocks that provide very uncertain rates of return. Although in an overall sense these investments are very risky, in some respects they may actually subject their owners to a reduced degree of certain varieties of risk. For example, the risk of losing real value in an investment during a period of unusually rapid price inflation is less for owners of gold and silver than it is for the owners of Treasury securities. Despite this, precious metals have a much less predictable return than short-term Treasury securities and, as a result, are significantly more risky.

One method of exploring the spectrum of risks among investment alternatives is with the risk-return graph of Exhibit 1–2. The graph's vertical axis measures expected rates of return, while the horizontal axis is scaled to indicate the relative uncertainty of return. The risk-return attributes of the various investments plotted indicate the relative position of one investment with another. The positively sloped curve indicates that investments with higher expected returns tend to have greater amounts of risk. For example, common stocks tend to be riskier and to produce higher expected returns than corporate bonds, which, in turn, produce higher expected returns and have a higher degree of risk than U.S. Government bonds.

Several important issues are relevant to the risk-return relationship of Exhibit 1–2. First, there is no reason to expect that the slope of the curve, which measures the additional return that investors demand in order to accept more risk, is static. If investors experience an increasing concern about risk, there is every reason to expect that they will demand increased premiums from investments they view as risky. This may occur, for example, if there is concern that a recent slowing in economic growth may eventually

Figure 1-2
Risk and Expected Return

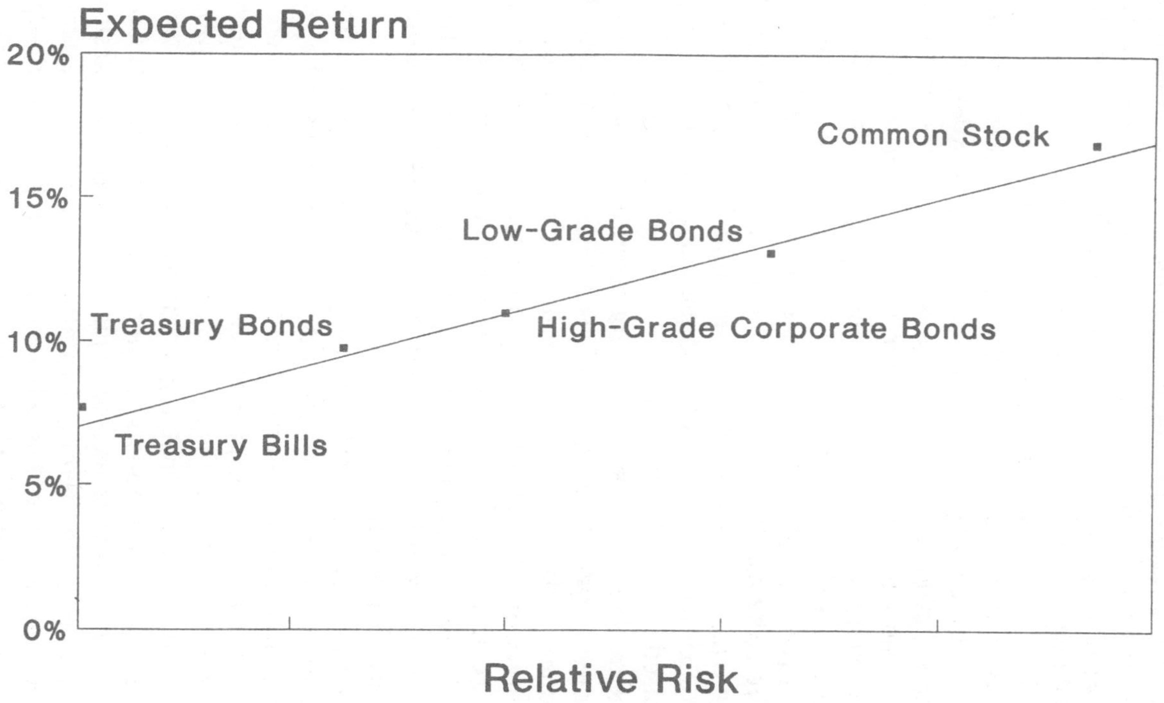

Expected Return

20%

15%

10%

5%

0%

Common Stock

Low-Grade Bonds

High-Grade Corporate Bonds

Treasury Bonds

Treasury Bills

Relative Risk

turn into a serious slump. The investment community might also experience increasing concern about investments of all types when confronted with unfavorable news about government deficits, trade deficits, unemployment, or a nearly infinite number of other grim news items.

During periods of uncertainty investors tend to seek safe havens such as insured certificates of deposit and Treasury securities. At the same time that these low-risk investments experience increased demand, junk bonds, speculative common stocks, and other high-risk investments lose their luster and fall in price as investors attempt to eliminate these assets from their portfolios. The attempt to dispose of risky investments will decrease the market prices of these investments as investors demand higher yields in order to acquire risky assets. This change in the market will rotate the risk-return curve counterclockwise and thereby increase the curve's slope. Exhibit 1–3 displays the adjustment of the curve to reflect an increased concern by investors.

One method of assessing investor attitudes toward risk is to track the interest rate differential between high-grade and medium- or low-grade debt securities. A reduced yield differential indicates that investors are not demanding much additional return for more risky bonds, thus demonstrating a decreased concern about risk. Conversely, if the spread widens between the two yields, it indicates that investors are viewing the investment horizon with increasing skepticism.

In addition to a constantly changing slope, upward and downward shifts may occur. Shifts in the curve are caused by changes in the risk-free rate of return. A reduction in the risk-free rate will result in a new curve at a lower level, while an increase in the risk-free rate will shift the curve upward. A parallel upward shift of the curve illustrates that higher interest rates affect virtually all investments in a negative manner. As the risk-return curve shifts upward, all investments will adjust in market value to provide the new, higher yields required to attract investment capital at their respective risk levels. There is no reason to expect that suppliers of investment capital will be willing to invest at former rates after the return on riskless investments increases.

Exhibit 1-3
Changes in the Risk-Return Relationship

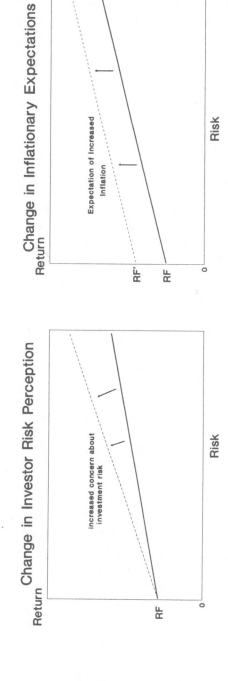

Change in Investor Risk Perception

Return

RF

increased concern about investment risk

0

Risk

Change in Inflationary Expectations

Return

RF'

RF

Expectation of Increased Inflation

0

Risk

If the increased risk-free rate is accompanied by heightened investor concern about risk, the curve will actually rotate counterclockwise at the same time it shifts upward, thereby producing a double dose of trouble for investments viewed as being unusually risky. An upward shift in the risk-return curve is displayed on the right side of Exhibit 1–3. The risk-free rate is shown in the diagram as RF prior to the shift and as RF′ subsequent to the shift.

THE IMPORTANCE OF EXPECTED INFLATION

The expected rate of price inflation is one of the major determinants of the rate of return on riskless investments. Inflation is a driving force in moving yields on all types of investments because both suppliers and users of funds factor this important variable into their evaluation of an investment agreement.

An investment's return adjusted for expected inflation is termed the "real" rate of return. This inflation-adjusted measure is in contrast to the nominal rate of return that is not adjusted for inflation. An investor earning an annual return of 8 percent on a three-year certificate of deposit during a time when price inflation averages 5 percent is earning a real rate of return of 3 percent. Only when consumer prices are not changing are the real and nominal rates equal.

An investment's estimated real return, not its nominal or stated return, is important to investors. An investor can judge the adequacy of an expected return only when there is some assumption about the rate of price inflation that will occur over the term of the investment. Investing funds at an expected return that is less than the rate of inflation is a losing proposition. When the rate of inflation is higher than an investment's return, the sum of the earnings and the returned principal have less purchasing power than did the original principal at the time investment was undertaken.

Even though investors incorporate an inflation factor in the returns they demand on investment assets, the rate of inflation will sometimes exceed an investment's return. The reason is that expected inflation, not actual inflation, is considered when funds are invested. Investors, like everyone else, frequently misjudge inflation—a mistake that can have serious consequences. For example, in 1988 a bond matured that had been issued by a corporation 40 years earlier. The fact that the bond carried a coupon interest rate of only 3 ¾ percent demonstrates that investors in the late 1940s certainly did not expect inflation to reach the unusually high levels experienced in the 1960s and 1970s.

The bottom line is that increases in expected inflation push the risk-return curve upward because investors demand higher nominal rates of return for all investments. If inflationary expectations rise dramatically, investors will demand higher returns from Treasury bills, corporate bonds, common stocks, real estate, and precious metals. Accepting an annual rate of return of 14 percent on a rental property when inflation is expected to be 4 percent is one thing. Accepting the same 14 percent rate of return when inflation is 15 percent is something else entirely.

Unless some way exists for an investment's cash flows (including cash from an eventual sale of the asset) to increase, the only way that an investment can adjust to provide a higher expected return is to fall in price. Thus, most investment vehicles adjust downward in price in order to provide new buyers with expected returns at higher levels. An investor may pay $300,000 for an investment that produces an annual cash flow of $30,000 when the rate of inflation is 4 percent. If the rate of inflation increases to 12 percent, investors will begin demanding increasingly higher returns to justify parting with their investment funds. If the higher inflation rate produces a market in which investors can earn 15 percent on similar assets, then the investment that was purchased for $300,000 must fall significantly in price in order to be marketable in the new inflationary environment.

Just as increases in expected inflation result in increases in the risk-free rate of return and are generally unfavorable for investments, reductions in expected inflation have the opposite effect of reducing the risk-free rate. The dramatic reduction in inflationary expectations during the early 1980s resulted in a substantial reduction in the returns provided by risk-free investments. This reduction, in turn, produced dramatic reductions in the rates of return that investors demanded from investments at all risk levels.

Inflationary expectations have a direct effect on investments as well as the indirect effect that operates through changes in interest rates. For example, an investor might make the case that inflation actually benefits the owners of gold and silver. This may be true, of course, but it is a separate issue. The increased returns (an upward shift in the curve) brought about by an increase in inflationary expectations has a negative effect on all investments including those of a tangible nature. At the same time, some investments may benefit from higher inflation because their payouts tend to increase during periods of rising consumer prices.

THE CAPACITY TO ASSUME RISK

The capacity of an investor to assume uncertain returns depends on a variety of variables peculiar to each individual. Age, income, financial responsibilities, and the amount and types of other owned assets are all relevant considerations in determining the acceptable level of risk in an investment. In general, the younger the age, the greater the value and the lower the risk of assets that are already held, the fewer the financial responsibilities, and the larger a person's income-earning capacity, the more risky will be the investment an investor may wish to acquire. All of these variables are important and should be considered in a properly managed investment program.

Age

Age is an important consideration in the ability to absorb risk, because it is a major determinant of an individual's future income-earning capacity. A young person looking forward to many years of earned income is in a much better position to recover from investment losses than is someone approaching retirement age. This ability to recover from investment losses means that a younger person can rationally select more risky investments in an attempt to earn returns higher than are available on low-risk investments.

The greater capacity to assume risk does not imply that all individuals under 40 years of age should seek high-risk investments. A number of considerations other than age must be included in the process of selecting investments. However, independent of these other factors, a younger age confers considerable flexibility as to the types of investments that may be selected.

An individual who has most of his years of job-related income behind him must necessarily be relatively conservative in selecting investments because of a lack of time to recover from losses. Choosing investments that entail considerable uncertainty makes little sense for someone who will soon be relying on a minimum level of investment income to cover living expenses. Losing 50 percent of one's life savings on a sour real estate deal at age 35 has entirely different consequences than losing 50 percent of one's life savings in several risky stock investments at age 64.

The Value of Assets That Are Owned

As a general rule, the greater the value of assets already owned, the greater the risk an investor can assume. This doesn't mean that a tidy nest egg makes it prudent to go out and shoot the moon on some long-shot investment. It does mean that a person can begin making riskier investment selections once a portfolio of assets has already been assembled. A person who has significant assets to fall back on is not affected nearly so much by widely varying rates of return on a new investment as is a person who possesses only a small portfolio of assets. Thus, a person who has amassed a sizable portfolio can seek out riskier investments with higher expected returns.

At the opposite end of the wealth scale, an individual with only a meager accumulation of assets is not in a position to assume much risk. In fact, a lack of assets is such an important consideration that it is a limiting factor for risk exposure no matter what other circumstances apply. Even a young or middle-aged investor should seek relatively low-risk assets until an investment portfolio of at least a modest value has been established.

The Types of Assets That Are Owned

A crucial consideration in any investor's investment selection is the types of assets that are already being held. For example, if an individual holds a very conservative portfolio of investments, there may be considerable freedom to acquire additional assets that have above-average risks. For an investor who owns fairly risky investments, it may be advisable to add new assets that have a greater certainty of return.

While nearly all types of assets are subject to some uncertainty of return, this uncertainty is not always affected by the same forces. For example, gold bullion and junk bonds are each considered to be fairly risky investments because there is substantial uncertainty surrounding the returns on each asset. However, the uncertainty relevant to each investment is the result of strikingly different factors. Events such as inflation and political strife would tend to push gold prices upward at the same time that they nudge junk bond prices downward. Conversely, a period of prosperity and strong economic expansion could prove to be a favorable development for holders of junk bonds while it might very well be harmful to investors with holdings of gold and the common stocks of firms that have an interest in gold.

Because fluctuations in the rates of return of various investments are influenced by different factors, two or more investments can be selectively combined to produce a portfolio risk that is less than the risk of either investment considered in isolation. Thus, an investor can acquire an investment that entails considerable risk if that risk will combine with the risks of assets already owned to produce a lower portfolio risk. For example, an investor with a portfolio comprising primarily financial assets might wish to add tangible assets in order to moderate overall risk.

Financial Responsibilities

An investor's financial responsibilities assume a major role in limiting the riskiness of investments. The greater the financial responsibilities a person must shoulder, the less uncertainty of return that should be accepted. Conversely, a person with very limited financial responsibilities has more freedom to select investments that entail considerable return uncertainty.

A common financial responsibility is having one or more individuals dependent for financial support upon someone else. These dependents could be young children, aged parents, or an incapacitated spouse. The fact that someone else who is unable to provide his or her own support is dependent upon another's income means that the income stream needs to be both adequate and certain. If investment income is counted upon to provide a portion of the required support, there may be little room for investments with uncertain returns. The greater the proportion of income that is provided by the investments (as opposed to income that is earned), the greater the desired certainty of return.

An individual with few financial responsibilities is in a position to acquire investments that have relatively high expected returns at the expense of considerable uncertainty. If the actual return from the investment turns out to be considerably less than expected, the loss is generally something that can be lived with.

Income-Earning Capacity

An investor with either a high current income or the capability to earn a high income if required is generally able to tolerate assets with relatively high degrees of risk. For example, a business executive with a secure job and a large salary can rationally acquire more risky investments than can someone who barely earns enough income to make ends meet. An individual with a modest earned income and no real prospect that the income will increase significantly should seek conservative investments. This individual should concentrate on investments that pay high current returns and that do so with the least uncertainty.

Not only current income, but also expected future income and the ability to earn income should be considered in selecting appropriate investments. An individual who has a limited amount of current income but who is reasonably certain of substantial future increases in income can afford to select investments with at least a moderate degree of risk in an attempt to earn higher expected rates of return. An example might be someone who has just graduated from medical school with a degree in a high-demand, high-income specialty area. The individual does not yet have a lucrative practice but little doubt exists that it will not be long before a relatively large income base will be established. Likewise, a person who is for whatever reason, working only part-time but who could easily return to full-time employment could seek more risky investments than earned income alone would tend to indicate was proper.

THE INDIVIDUAL INVESTOR AS A RISKY ASSET

One of the most valuable financial assets that most people possess is their own ability to generate income. For the majority of individuals, this flow of income is unsurpassed by the income produced by any other asset and, frequently, by all of their other assets combined. An individual earning $40,000 per year from employment would require assets of between $400,000 and $500,000 in order to produce the same amount of before-tax income with the same degree of certainty. Even then, these assets would have to be of the variety that pay most of their return in current dividends or interest. Also, earned income tends to adjust for changes in consumer prices through annual raises. This is a luxury that few low-risk investments confer.

The importance of one's ability to produce earned income requires that any assessment of an individual's investment portfolio include the individual as a component. Not doing so presents an incomplete picture of the capacity to handle risky investments and leaves the individual vulnerable to making faulty investment decisions.

Factors that affect the value of an individual's ability to produce income are the same as those that influence the value of any asset. For example, the amount of annual earnings, the number of years during which the person will continue to work and produce income, and the stability of the income are all material considerations. It is important that fringe benefits also be considered. Medical insurance, life insurance, and an employer's contributions to a vested pension plan are each very important components of earned income, even if they aren't always taxed as such.

The larger the relative importance of one's employment income in combination with a greater uncertainty of that income (as, for example, if an individual's skills are so specialized that it would be difficult to locate similar employment at a comparable salary), the lower the capacity for being subject to doubtful returns from investments. Uncertain employment means that the most valuable asset that the individual owns is very risky in the sense that earned income is quite tentative. This risk needs to be balanced with investments that produce a reliable return. At the other extreme, a person with a very secure job (e.g., an executive with a substantial "golden parachute") can invest in assets that have significant amounts of risk.

VIEWING RISK IN A COMPREHENSIVE FRAMEWORK

As various risks are examined in Chapters 2 and 3, it will be pointed out that certain of these risks are interrelated while other risks operate independently of one another. Understanding how the uncertainties of owning various assets may be linked is important in pursuing a program of controlling risk, because it permits an investor to view an asset in terms of how it will affect an existing portfolio. For example, uncertain returns caused by changing interest rates and by unexpected inflation are so closely related that it is generally unwise to select an investment that is subject to a great uncertainty of returns from rising interest rates when the investor has a portfolio subject to significant risk from unexpected inflation.

An inability or unwillingness to examine risk in a comprehensive framework is a failing of many individuals. Investors frequently select an investment on what they view as the investment's own merits and weaknesses without considering how the asset's acquisition or sale will affect the riskiness of their entire investment portfolio.

Combining assets having similar risk characteristics produces a risky investment portfolio. Combining assets having diverse risk characteristics results in an investment portfolio with less total risk than the risks of its components. The greater the number of assets and the more dissimilar their respective uncertainties, the less risky a portfolio becomes. On the other hand, a large number of assets that have virtually identical risks (i.e., a portfolio composed solely of petroleum-related common stocks or of long-term debt securities) results in an investment position that has nearly as much risk as its individual components.

Three crucial concerns must be addressed to cope with risk in a comprehensive manner. The first is why rates of return may turn out to be different from what is expected. This involves identifying the types of risks investors face. Chapters 2 and 3 will be devoted to this task.

The next task is to recognize risks inherent in owning a particular type of investment. For example, how is the rate of return from the ownership of gold influenced by interest rates, by inflation, or by changes in economic activity? To what extent is the rate of return from owning the common stock of an electric utility affected by these same factors? The types of risks involved in owning individual investments will be covered in Chapters 4 through 6.

The third consideration is the degree to which the different risks of various investments are related. For instance, are the rates of return on gold bullion and long-term corporate bonds influenced by the same factors? If so, to what extent? Are the returns from owning precious metals and the common stocks of high-tech firms afflicted with similar uncertainties? It is the relationships among these risks that determines how investments interrelate in a portfolio.

SELF-HELP QUESTIONS

1. Suppose you have the following investment alternatives. Investment A is very safe and promises an annual return of 7 percent for five years. You have no doubt that the return will be earned and that you will have your principal repaid. Investment B has an expected return of 7 percent but you estimate that the actual return could range between 1 percent and 13 percent annually for four years. Which alternative would you choose?

   If Investment B has an expected return of 7 percent but a range of possible annual returns of from minus 5 percent to plus 19 percent, would your answer change? Are there any other details of the investment that you would like to have before making a decision?

2. What is the current risk-free return available to investors such as yourself? How does this compare with the returns you are earning on your current investments? Of the current risk-free return, how much is a result of expected inflation?

3. With respect to your age, assets, and existing financial responsibilities, how do you judge your capacity to assume

risk? Which of these are most important in limiting your ability to asssume risk in selecting investments?

4. Comparing yourself to a brother, sister, or close friend, how do you view your capacity to assume risk as different from theirs?

5. On a scale of 1 to 10, with 1 being someone who avoids investment risk at all costs and 10 being someone who seeks risky investments, where would you place yourself? How does this ranking correspond to your answer to question 4?

6. How do your current investments correspond to your answer to question 5? In surveying your current assets do you feel that your new investments should be either more or less risky than those that you already own?

Chapter
Two

RISKS ENCOUNTERED
BY INVESTORS

At some point an investor will experience the consequences of risks either knowingly or unknowingly assumed from the purchase of investment assets. The risks can be identified and the consequences planned for prior to when they actually occur or the risks and potential consequences can simply be ignored. As many investors have learned to their regret, the latter option can bring some very unpleasant repercussions.

The events causing uncertain investment returns are so numerous and varied that identifying them all presents a challenge to even the most experienced and sophisticated investors. For simplicity's sake, it is useful to classify risks into broad groups according to their effects upon investments. For example, the risk that price inflation will eat away at an investment's real returns is actually an aggregate of an almost unlimited number of possible occurrences, including oil embargoes, droughts, labor shortages, large increases in the money supply, declining values for the dollar in relation to foreign currencies, and so forth. Generalizing about the results of these events makes it possible to develop a manageable set of alternatives that enable an investor to formulate a plan of action to control risk.

With an understanding of the types of risks applicable to particular assets, an investor can select individual investments and combinations of investments that have the lowest risk exposure to the types of events the investor considers most damaging. If an individual's greatest concern is an unexpected increase in inflation, for example, it is prudent to devise an investment strategy that addresses this hazard. On the other hand, if quick access to cash is a major concern, it is important to choose investments that provide maximum liquidity.

CATEGORIES OF RISK

The causes of uncertain investment returns can be grouped into two very broad categories: events that affect virtually all investment assets and events that produce effects more applicable to specific investments or categories of investments. For example, inflation tends to influence the returns on virtually all investments. Even common stock, an asset frequently touted as an inflation hedge, provides returns that are affected by changes in the prices of goods and services. On the other hand, reliance on borrowed money is a function of an organization's management policy. Thus, the possible inability to meet financial obligations is a risk applicable to specific assets.

Some investments are mostly swayed by the broad forces of the first category and provide rates of return heavily influenced by changes in market currents. The uncertainties of these returns depend greatly on market forces. Other investments are affected by overall market movements to a much smaller extent and seem to experience lives of their own. Investments in the latter category produce rates of return heavily dependent upon unique factors and, in some cases, may have returns negatively correlated to market returns. For example, precious metals often produce positive investment returns at the same time that most investments are mired in a bear market.

Certain kinds of events tend to affect all sectors of business, government, and virtually any other entity, and produce unavoidable effects for an investor. Universally applicable uncertainties fall under a common classification known as systematic risk.

These risks can be influenced by an investor but cannot be completely eliminated. Two important systematic risks are the uncertain returns caused by uncertain purchasing power and uncertain interest rates. Uncertainties originating from both of these risks affect all investments to differing degrees.

Unsystematic risk includes uncertainties peculiar to an individual organization or investment. Risks of this nature can be minimized or even avoided altogether by careful investment selection. That is, unsystematic risks can be avoided or significantly reduced if the investor understands what the risks are and which types of investments tend to carry specific risks. Among the risks classified as unique are uncertain business factors that relate to a specific firm or industry, large amounts of fixed obligations such as lease and interest payments, and difficulty in converting an investment into cash.

PURCHASING-POWER RISK

Purchasing-power risk refers to the uncertainty of an investment's real rate of return as a result of inflation. The risk to an investor is that periodic income from sources such as dividends, interest, and rent payments, along with the funds eventually received when the investment is sold will be depleted in real value by increased prices for goods and services.

Purchasing-power risk is an uncertainty of major importance for many investors. Individuals who depend on investment income to meet living expenses may discover that inflation substantially erodes the quantity and quality of the goods and services they are able to purchase. Anyone who retired prior to the 1970s on a fixed monthly income can speak volumes about the inadequacy of a retirement income that once seemed generous. Likewise, individuals who invest to realize a specific objective will find that the amount of money needed to achieve the objective continually changes because of reduced purchasing power. One merely needs to observe what has happened to the cost of four years of college education to grasp the potential difficulty of successfully meeting an important financial goal.

There is another side to inflation that was discussed in Chapter 1. That is, unexpected inflation often brings about the anticipation of even more inflation in the future. This, in turn, pushes interest rates upward and asset values downward. Thus, inflation can produce a double whammy for investors; increased interest rates force the market value of investments downward at the same time that higher prices for goods and services reduce the purchasing power of the depleted dollar value. The effect of interest rates on investment risk will be discussed later in this chapter.

Inflation Estimates and Investment Values

The previous chapter showed that investment prices and expected returns incorporate a consensus expectation of future price inflation. The expected level of inflation is incorporated into the market values of investments when investors judge the asset's market value on the basis of the real, or inflation-adjusted, returns that are expected. The market prices of gold, stocks, bonds, and real estate are each affected by the inflationary expectations of market participants. As these expectations are altered, the market prices of most investment assets will change.

Because expected inflation is factored into an asset's market value, the real uncertainty that investors face is inflation at a level other than the expected rate. Suppose that a certificate of deposit with a five-year maturity yields 9 percent at a time when investors are expecting price inflation to average 6 percent. Someone who purchases this certificate expects to earn a real return before taxes of 3 percent, the difference between the quoted yield and the expected inflation rate. If the inflation rate proves to be either higher or lower than the expected level, the real return will be different than 3 percent. For example, if the prices for goods and services stabilize such that inflation is actually zero over the time that the certificate is held, the real return will be an unexpectedly high 9 percent annually. This will be a bonanza for the investor who purchased the certificate but, in real terms, it is considerably more costly than the seller anticipated. Only if the inflation rate actually proves to be the expected 6 percent annually does the certificate provide a real return to the investor and a real cost to the issuer that the market expected at the time the certificate was issued.

The extent to which investments subject their owners to uncertainty from unexpected inflation varies a great deal. Investments that provide a flow of cash that fails to adjust for shifts in inflation produce the greatest losses. For example, long-term bonds with fixed principal and semi-annual interest payments can subject investors to substantial declines in real returns if the inflation rate is higher than the level expected when the bonds were purchased. On the other hand, some investments such as precious metals generally thrive on news of unexpected inflation. Thus, values of this group of investments may actually be helped by rising prices for goods and services.

The Unpredictability of Inflation

Although the United States has not experienced the hyperinflation suffered in many other countries, the rate of inflation in consumer goods and services has nonetheless fluctuated widely. History seems to relate that the economy cycles through alternating periods of relatively stable prices followed by periods of rapidly escalating prices. The years of inflation are eventually succeeded by more years of comparative price stability as government officials feel the heat of public discord and become concerned enough to take the painful actions that will moderate price increases.

In recent years, a period commencing in the mid-1970s and running through the latter 1980s provides a classic example of a relatively sudden reversal of inflation and of inflationary expectations. During this span of time unexpected price stability followed on the heels of several years of unusually severe inflation. Exhibit 2–1 illustrates that the level of inflation as measured by the gross national product price deflator fluctuated in a range of from 6.5 percent to nearly 10 percent annually for a decade before dropping below 4 percent in the mid-1980s. The consumer price index (CPI), an inferior but more frequently quoted measure of inflation, ranged between 13.5 percent and 1.9 percent during this same period. What is especially notable is the suddenness with which the turnaround in inflation occurred. Even the most optimistic of forecasters had not expected that price increases could be subdued so quickly.

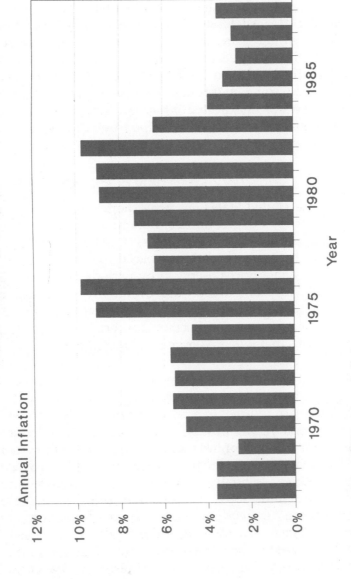

Exhibit 2-1
Annual Inflation, 1967-1989

Annual Inflation

Measured using GNP price deflator

Despite the importance of inflationary expectations, investors find that inflation is difficult to estimate, especially in the long run, because price changes are influenced by so many forces that are themselves difficult to forecast. Even professional economists and government officials who make a living from analyzing and projecting economic variables find that their estimates of inflation are frequently inaccurate.

Factors as unpredictable as the weather and political upheavals in foreign countries can have major impacts on consumer prices. One need only recall the effects of unusual weather conditions on food prices and the series of oil price shocks on energy costs to realize that the inflation rate can be quite fickle. Nearly every experienced economic forecaster feels a need to hedge an inflation forecast, not because the factors influencing prices are not understood, but because of an acknowledged inability to foresee the future course in each of the events that can affect prices.

With inflation so volatile and difficult to predict, changes in inflation become the rule rather than the exception. This, in turn, makes it difficult for investors to determine if an expected return is sufficient to offset the effects of potential declines in purchasing power. The more difficult it is to accurately incorporate inflation into investment planning the more risk the investor faces, because the more likely it is that expected investment returns are off target.

Investment Attributes That Reduce Purchasing-Power Risk

Purchasing-power risk from owning various investments ranges from nearly nonexistent to very high. Some investments subject their owners to only minor uncertainties from inflation, while other investments have substantial uncertainties regarding the real returns that will be realized. The great variation in risks among the various types of investments suggests that an investor can exercise a degree of control over purchasing-power risk by exercising judgment in the selection of assets. The question that must be addressed is: what attributes tend to make an investment resistant to the ravages of inflation?

An investment that returns an investor's cash in the shortest possible time will be little affected by changes in purchasing power. An
example is an asset in which the principal is scheduled to be
returned in a matter of days after the investment is made. Short of
several days of hyperinflation of an unbelievable magnitude, inflation will be inconsequential in affecting the purchasing power of
the investment's cash flow. Even investments requiring holding
periods of several weeks or several months tend to be unaffected by
changes in consumer prices in inflationary environments that have
prevailed in most developed countries.

Purchasing-power risk is also a function of the extent to which an
investment's payments are influenced by changing consumer
prices. The more an investment's cash flows and market value are
directly correlated with the level of consumer prices, the less the
purchasing-power risk from owning the asset. If an investment's
payments change to compensate its owner for any changes in the
prices of goods and services, the real return from holding the investment remains unaffected by inflation.

Suppose an investment pays an annual return of 3 percent, which
is adjusted upward for any inflation and downward for any defla-
tion. Investors holding the asset will be sheltered from purchasing-
power risk through recurring changes in the nominal return.
Regardless of the inflation that actually takes place, cash payments—either periodic income or the principal—are adjusted to offset changes in consumer prices. Thus, if consumer prices decline by
2 percent during a year, the nominal return that year will be
reduced to 1 percent. Any investment that promises an inflation-adjusted, or a real rate of return, shields its owner from purchasing-
power risk.

Even when there is no guarantee but only the expectation that the
nominal return will adjust for inflation, the investment will at least
partially compensate an investor for unanticipated changes in inflation or inflationary expectations. An example of such an asset might
be an ownership position in a business that is generally able to pass
along price increases to its customers. The relationship between
investment returns and inflation is spotty but still direct, so that the
investor is partially protected against purchasing-power risk.

How Purchasing-Power Risk Varies among Investments

Investments with variable payments that are directly correlated with inflation are not always easy to identify. Short-term investments such as money-market accounts and Treasury bills fit this mold because, as Chapter 1 pointed out, short-term interest rates tend to be directly influenced by the rate of inflation. Thus, increased inflation will push interest rates upward, so that when the time comes to reinvest capital, the investor will be able to earn a higher nominal return.

Some corporations are able to take advantage of an inflationary period to pass along price increases to customers. The increased revenues that result are likely to produce additional profits and dividends to stockholders. This ability of corporations to increase profits during inflation is not universal, however, so that common stocks and direct ownership of businesses are not always good inflation hedges.

In general, eventual cash payments from the resale of tangible investments such as precious metals and real estate can be expected to benefit from inflation. These investments tend to increase in value during inflationary periods, so that when the assets are sold, their market values will have adjusted at least partially to compensate the owner for inflation during the holding period.

The relationship between asset values and the level of consumer prices is, at best, tentative. Investors sometimes purchase tangible assets only to find that these assets decline in market value despite an increase in consumer prices. The reason is that changing market values for tangible assets are more a function of changing expectations of inflation, not simply the current level of inflation. If investors feel that inflation has peaked, then the prices of tangible assets may fall despite the fact that inflation may continue, but at a reduced level.

Gold and silver are priced with the expectation of some level of inflation. If inflation occurs as expected, these assets have been accurately valued on the basis of investors' assumptions about price inflation. If, however, inflationary expectations prove to have been too low, the market prices of gold and silver are likely to rise.

Conversely, if investors have overestimated inflation, precious metals are likely to adjust downward in price.

As a rule, long-term, fixed-payment investments have substantial amounts of purchasing-power risk. These investments have an expected level of inflation built into the original price, but once funds are committed to the investment, no adjustments will occur to compensate investors for unexpected inflation. Long-term bonds of all kinds, annuity contracts with fixed returns, retirement plans with fixed payouts and long-term certificates of deposit, all subject their owners to significant amounts of uncertainty in real rates of return because of an unpredictability of future changes in consumer prices.

The possibility always exists that inflation will be lower than the market anticipates. This scenario turns everything topsy-turvy and would benefit the owners of long-term investments with fixed payments. An example of such a bonanza occurred for buyers of long-term bonds during the early 1980s when the financial markets anticipated a continuation of the high inflation rates then in progress (see Exhibit 2–1). These bonds had substantial inflationary expectations included in their yields and, thus, carried very high coupon rates. To the surprise of nearly everyone except perhaps President Reagan, inflation subsided significantly only a few years later, so that investors who had purchased bonds during the pessimistic years of the early 1980s earned real rates of return that were significantly higher than all but the most optimistic of them had anticipated.

While a reduction in inflationary expectations is good for investments with fixed cash flows, it may result in reduced cash flows and market values for investments that provide returns that are directly linked to inflation. For example, tangible assets generally perform very poorly during periods of declining or stable prices. Because of the way investments are valued in the marketplace, assets that normally benefit from rising inflationary expectations will be harmed by reduced inflationary expectations. Thus, there is purchasing-power risk with tangible investments, but the relationship that exists between asset values and inflation is turned upside down.

INTEREST-RATE RISK

Interest-rate risk refers to the uncertain returns caused by uncertain market rates of interest. The risk to the investor is that an investment's return will be adversely affected by changes in interest rates during the period the investment is held. The more an investment's rate of return is influenced by changes in interest rates, the greater the uncertainty surrounding the return and the larger the interest-rate risk from owning that investment.

Unlike inflation, which reduces the purchasing power of the cash received from owning an investment, interest-rate changes frequently produce changes in the size of the cash payments or, more likely, in the market value of the investment. Interestingly, the risks investors assume with respect to interest rates (that current income will fall and that market values will be adversely affected) are outcomes generally applicable to two very different types of investments.

Changing cash payments are a risk of investments that have payments keyed to some current interest rate or to some other variable that is a function of interest rates. Changing market values tend to be a risk inherent in investments that provide their owners with fixed cash payments. For some investments, changing interest rates may influence current income payments at the same time they affect market value. The common thread running through all of these assets is that an investor owning any of them will face an uncertain rate of return because of potential changes in interest rates.

First, consider an investment with payouts keyed directly to some interest-rate standard, say the yield on a specific issue of Treasury securities. Each scheduled payment from the investment will change depending on changes that have occured in the interest rate used as the standard. Thus, if the interest-rate standard rises, payments to the investment's owner will increase. Alternatively, if the standard declines, the payments will be reduced. The problem for the investor is that unless some way exists to accurately forecast interest rates, there is no way of determining in advance what will happen to the size of the investment's income flow. Knowing with some degree of certainty the flow of income to be provided by an investment is especially important for someone who depends on the current income from an investment to meet a large portion of current spending needs.

The second type of interest-rate risk relates to the extent that changing interest rates will produce changes in an investment's market value. If an investment's market value is a function of the level of interest rates, then an individual owning this investment will be subject to uncertain returns. Chapter 1 discussed the concept of how investment values can be affected by changes in the return on risk-free assets. As the risk-free return increases, the market value for most investments tends to fall. Thus, for investments that make payments independent of changes in market rates of interest, there is every reason to expect that an adjustment in market value must be made in order to make the investment competitive with yields on other investments.

The Volatility of Interest Rates

For many years interest-rate risk was no more than a minor concern for the majority of investors. Federal Reserve officials pursued a policy of promoting a relatively low and stable level of interest rates that tended to minimize the cost of government borrowing. This policy produced a financial environment in which individual investors worried little about interest-rate changes. Not until 1966 did the average yield on new three-month Treasury bills surpass 4 percent. Such a sanguine environment is difficult to imagine for investors who have come of age in the 1970s and 1980s, a period when interest rates have been extremely volatile. These large, rapid, and unpredictable fluctuations in interest rates have generated considerable uncertainty among investors who purchase interest-sensitive investments.

Short-term interest rates tend to be considerably more volatile than long-term interest rates. Specific short-term rates such as the federal funds rate, the rate on money-market mutual funds, the rate on Treasury bills, and the commercial paper rate are all subject to substantial movements in a relatively short time. Long-term rates such as those on mortgages and on corporate and government bonds with long maturities can be subject to sudden movements, but generally to a much smaller degree than the rates on short-term investments. During a time when the interest rate on six-month Treasury bills might move 3 or 4 percentage points, the rate on 30-year Treasury bonds might change no more than 1 or 2 percentage points.

In the early 1980s, short-term interest rates moved from an unusually high level, where they were actually higher than long-term rates, to a much reduced level, where they were below long-term rates. This dramatic movement in short-term interest rates occurred during a relatively short time. The difference in volatility of short-term and long-term interest rates is illustrated in Exhibit 2–2, which displays the annual ranges for the yields on Treasury bills and on long-term Treasury bonds.

Determinants of Interest Rates

Interest rates are influenced by the shifting winds from a wide variety of forces, many of which are extremely difficult to forecast. Among the numerous variables that affect both short-term and long-term interest rates are government deficits, the level of economic activity, trade balances between the U.S. and foreign countries, interest rates in other countries, and virtually anything that can influence investors' expectations regarding inflation.

One of the most important determinants of interest-rate levels is the monetary policy of the Federal Reserve. The Federal Reserve is governed by appointed members who have the power to alter the nation's money supply, an element crucial in determining interest rates. Periods of tight money, such as that experienced by the U.S. economy in the early 1980s, produced high interest rates that hammered the nation's financial markets and helped produce a severe recession. The Board's goal was to squeeze out a major part of the inflation that had been gaining strength since the latter 1960s. Inflation had become so ingrained in peoples' thinking and actions that the Federal Reserve needed to put significant pressure on the financial markets in order to alter expectations and bring price changes under control.

Because Federal Reserve policy is considered so important in setting the tone for inflation, interest rates, and investment values, the investment community closely monitors the actions of the Board.

Exhibit 2-2
Yields on Short- and Long-Term Bonds

3-Month Treasury Bills

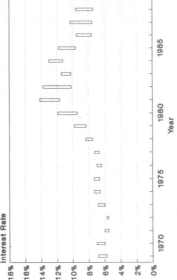

Long-Term Treasury Bonds

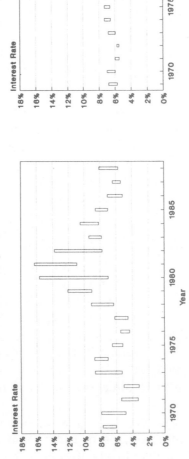

Changes in the federal funds rate, the fee that commercial banks charge one another to borrow reserves, is considered a key indicator of the Fed's current policy and of its future intentions. The federal funds rate is a measure of the tightness of commercial bank reserves, a variable that the Fed targets in its efforts to influence the economy. In an attempt to correctly anticipate future Board action, investors also closely monitor public comments by Federal Reserve members.

Federal Reserve actions to increase the money supply and make credit more abundant have the effect of pushing interest rates down in the short run, as lenders and borrowers find funds more plentiful. At the same time that short-term rates are falling from the increased availability of credit, investors may become concerned about added inflationary pressures over the longer term if they view increases in the money supply as excessive. Because long-term, fixed-income securities are so sensitive to inflationary expectations, long-term interest rates may increase at the same time short-term rates are falling.

The combination of short-run and long-run effects from Federal Reserve actions requires the Fed to walk a fine line in setting monetary policy. The Board must increase the money supply sufficiently to permit the credit expansion that allows economic growth, while not increasing it so much that the added supply of money produces pressure for price increases in consumer goods and services. In the opposite context, the Federal Reserve must not keep such a tight reign on the money supply that tight credit conditions and high interest rates choke the economy into a recession.

Investment Attributes That Reduce Interest-Rate Risk

Interest-rate uncertainties produce two very different risks for investors, the risk of uncertain returns because of uncertain cash flows and the risk of uncertain returns because of uncertain market values. Unfortunately, the attributes that tend to reduce one of these risks simultaneously tend to increase the other. Thus, investments that protect an investor from uncertain cash flows caused by interest-rate changes tend to produce substantial risk from uncertain market values. At the opposite extreme, investments that provide protection against uncertain market values caused by interest-rate changes subject the investor to substantial risk from uncertain cash flows.

The risk of uncertain income flows that are the result of interest-rate changes can best be avoided by selecting investments that guarantee fixed cash payments over long time periods. If the payments to be received by an investor are not a function of interest rates (other than at the time that the investment is acquired) then interest-rate changes, regardless of their direction or size, will have no effect on income flows provided by the investment. Retirees who depend on a constant income flow to meet current expenses generally find an asset of this type desirable to own.

The risk from potential changes in investment values caused by fluctuations in interest rates are best avoided by selecting long-term investments with payments altered to reflect market rates of interest or by restricting investment acquisitions to assets with short-term maturities. Of the two, short-term investments are in plentiful supply and a more appropriate alternative for most investors.

An investment that returns an investor's outlay in a short time is subject to very little change in value from fluctuations in interest rates. First, interest rates don't tend to change much during very short periods. Second, even if interest rates experience more than a relatively small change, the investor would soon have the principal returned and be able to reinvest the funds at the prevailing interest rate. Whenever an investment approaches the date when its principal is scheduled for return, the asset will have a market value nearly equal to the amount of money to be received. Thus, the market values of all types of short-term investments are relatively immune to changes in either short-term or long-term interest rates.

Investments with intermediate and long maturities can protect investors from value changes as a result of interest-rate changes if payments from the asset respond directly to interest-rate movements. For example, an asset that provides increased payments when interest rates rise and decreased payments when interest rates fall will protect an investor against changes in the market value of the investment when interest rates change. Essentially, this type of investment provides an income stream nearly identical to the flow of current income accruing to the owners of the short-term investments. Both types of investments provide fluctuating income keyed to the current level of interest rates.

How Interest-Rate Risk Varies among Investments

Assets providing an income flow that adjusts to changes in interest rates protect an investor from fluctuations in market value as a result of interest-rate changes. Short-term investments such as money-market funds, money-market accounts at banks and savings institutions, short-term certificates of deposit, and U.S. Treasury bills all meet this requirement. These assets mature in short time periods and, thus, permit the owner to reinvest the funds at whatever the market rate of interest happens to be at the time of the rollover. With these investments the principal is protected as the return fluctuates directly with interest rates.

Bonds and preferred stocks with floating dividends or interest make payments that are adjusted for the existing short-term interest rate at the time the payments are made. These floating-rate securities protect an investor from changes in market value, because they provide returns related to current interest rates. If rates rise, then payments rise accordingly; if rates decline, then payments decline. Regardless of the movement in interest rates, the return from the investment makes a corresponding change.

The downside of owning assets that produce cash payments that are a function of short-term interest rates is that they subject investors to considerable uncertainty regarding the amount of current income to be received. Although this risk is occasioned by changing interest rates, it is classified separately as reinvestment risk and will be discussed in more detail in the next chapter.

Long-term assets with fixed payment schedules, investments such as long-term bonds, preferred stock, long-term loan contracts, and many retirement plans, provide protection against the uncertain income flows that result from interest-rate changes. In most cases, these investments pay a fixed periodic sum regardless of what happens to the market level of interest rates. Thus, an investor locks in a fixed stream of payments and knows the exact amount of income each period. Because of their fixed payments, long-term bonds and preferred stocks vary considerably in market value as a result of changes in market rates of interest. This risk is especially important if an investor has reason to believe that an asset may have to be sold on short notice.

Some investments can have both a current income and a market value subject to variation because of changes in interest rates. In other words, if interest rates rise, then the asset's current income may decline along with its market value. An asset with both income and value that are affected in the same manner by interest-rate changes subjects investors to a great uncertainty of return. For example, a business involved in the construction of buildings will almost surely be adversely affected by rising interest rates. Higher interest rates will result in a decline in construction projects with the consequence of reduced sales, so that both current income in the form of profits and dividends and the value of the ownership will decline. The income of most utilities is adversely affected by rising interest rates, simply because these firms borrow so much money. Borrowing at higher rates penalizes profits and can endanger dividends to owners. Thus, the common stock of utilities subjects investors to significant amounts of risk from changing interest rates.

On the other hand, some firms can actually experience an increase in profits because of higher market rates of interest. The increased earnings and dividends may partially or completely offset any tendency for higher interest rates to decrease the firm's market value (or the market value of its common stock). Companies that have accumulated large cash positions may be able to increase their own profits when interest rates rise. These firms will be able to reinvest their short-term funds at higher interest rates and produce a larger current income for owners. Likewise, companies involved in lending money may discover that they can increase the interest rate on the funds they lend by more than the increase in their own cost of funds. Rising interest rates would produce higher profits for these firms.

The bottom line of interest-rate risk makes for bad reading: there is no easy way to completely avoid it. Investments that provide protection against uncertain returns in the form of changing current income flows subject their owners to the full effects of uncertain returns from changes in market value. On the other hand, investments that provide protection from the uncertain returns of changing market values tend to subject their owners to the full effects of uncertain returns from current income.

Although no investment possesses all the right attributes when it comes to protection against uncertain returns caused by interest-rate changes, there are investments that provide a compromise between stability of income and stability of market value. For example, intermediate-length investments such as five-year certificates of deposit or bonds with five- to seven-year maturities have a degree of uncertain market value, but not a lot. Likewise, assets that provide for a return of funds in five to seven years subject their owners to some uncertainty of income, because the funds received from the investment must be reinvested at a return unknown at the time the money is initially committed. On the positive side, the flow of income is at least guaranteed during the years until the funds must be reinvested.

SELF-HELP QUESTIONS

1. Considering the recent history of inflation illustrated in Exhibit 2–1, what do you think is the outlook for increases in the prices of goods and services over the next five years? The next decade?

2. How much protection will your investments provide against the inflation you expect? If inflation should be substantially higher than you expect, how will the return on your investments be affected? If inflation is substantially lower than you expect?

3. To what extent will your employment income respond to inflation? Do you feel that your earned income, adjusted for inflation, will increase over the next decade? How does this play a part in the selection of investment assets?

4. How are inflationary expectations incorporated into investment yields and market values? Why do changing expectations influence the market values of investment assets? Are any investments likely to be unaffected by changing inflationary expectations?

5. What part does the Federal Reserve play in influencing inter-
    est rates in the United States? Why is there political pressure
    on the Federal Reserve to keep interest rates low? What is the
    long-run outlook from such a policy?

6. If interest rates climbed substantially over the next year, how
    would the market values of your current investments be af-
    fected? If you knew that interest rates were going to rise,
    would you make any changes to your current investments
    portfolio?

7. If short-term interest rates are more volatile than long-term
    interest rates, why are short-term securities less volatile in
    price than long-term securities? Is your own portfolio of in-
    vestments tilted toward investments that are heavily affected
    by changes in interest rates?

Chapter
Three

RISKS ENCOUNTERED BY INVESTORS (CONTINUED)

Unexpected inflation and interest-rate changes are significant risks that affect virtually every asset, but they are certainly not the only causes of uncertain investment returns. This chapter will discuss additional risks that investors will encounter in their quest for investment income.

BUSINESS RISK

Business risk refers to an investment's uncertain returns because of the uncertain business environment in which the organization operates. This poor performance may be the result of unwise management decisions or inefficiencies in the delivery of products or services. It may also be caused by events external to the entity, such as a change in the value of the dollar relative to other currencies, which makes it difficult for a firm to compete. And there is always the possibility that a new competitor will emerge and knock the socks off a company that has been operating in a sheltered environment.

One could argue that uncertain rates of return caused by events such as these can more accurately be called organization risk. The risk is that an investment will produce volatile returns because of some uncertainty relative to the organization in which the investment is made.

Business risk is classified as unsystematic because it results from occurrences unique to a particular investment or to a particular organization. Because business risk is unique, the extent to which an investor is exposed to this risk varies significantly from one type of investment to another and is subject to being influenced by an investor's selection of assets.

The Many Causes of Business Risk

Business risk is so diverse and widespread simply because there are so many ways an organization can experience adversity. Even the largest and oldest organizations are subject to being decimated by a single event or by a series of unfavorable events. Such a giant company as PennCentral, a combination of the Pennsylvania and the New York Central railroads, declared bankruptcy in the early 1970s after years as one of the blue-chip firms of American business. The decade of the 1980s experienced its own spectacular and equally improbable failure, when Washington Public Power Supply System, a huge not-for-profit regional electric utility, became a victim of reduced energy demand, broken contracts by customers for the purchase of electricity, and its own faulty growth estimates. The giant public utility declared bankruptcy and defaulted on $2.25 billion in debt. The reasons behind these two mammoth bankruptcies were very different, but investors in both organizations lost billions of dollars.

Investments in personal businesses or in the securities of public corporations are subject to business risk that varies greatly from firm to firm. For example, a company that depends on a single product for most of its revenues may discover that demand for that product unexpectedly begins to languish. A new and superior competing product may usurp demand for the firm's output, or (as in the case of the hula hoop and many clothing fashions) the public may simply tire of using the product or of having it around. As a result of the oil shocks that took place twice during the 1970s, automobile manufacturers had a very difficult time selling large gas-guzzling vehicles. The demand for big cars eventually recovered, but the decline in sales, although temporary, was quite severe. The aftermath of the oil shocks brought a glut of oil with plummeting prices and resulting bankruptcies for many of the industry's firms that were prospering only a few years earlier.

Even an asset generally considered to be a fairly consistent producer of stable cash flows, rental real estate, is subject to business risk. Neighborhoods deteriorate and entire geographic regions routinely go through periods of overbuilding. The result is homes, apartments, and office buildings that can be rented only at reduced rates or, in the most unfavorable environments, not at all. Towns and regions can suffer economic downturns that continue for decades.

The diversity and unpredictability of the events described above demonstrate how devastating business risk can be to investors. Unlike purchasing-power risk, which tends to eat away at income and asset values over a period of years, and interest-rate risk, which may produce a significant loss but generally not one of terminal size, business risk can produce huge losses in a relatively short time. The oil industry is perhaps the premier example of such a riches to rags story. From immense profitability in which many firms had difficulty in deciding what to do with their immense amounts of cash, many companies plummeted into bankruptcy in a matter of only a few years. Owners and creditors alike saw their investments evaporate because of adversity peculiar to the industry.

Even government entities can be subject to business risk. State and local governments may be hit by an economic recession that results in lower tax revenues and a reduced ability to provide services to their citizens. Large cities may find their economic base deteriorating as companies seek new locations and many well-heeled citizens move to the suburbs. Expensive public projects such as toll roads, toll bridges, and electric generating systems may be constructed, only to find that planners grossly overestimated the need for the good or service the project was designed to deliver.

Investments That Reduce Business Risk

One method of avoiding the uncertain returns caused by business risk is to stick to obligations guaranteed by the federal government. Most U.S. Government obligations subject investors to certain risks, including purchasing-power risk and interest-rate risk, but these investments are generally considered to be free of business risk. This assumes, of course, that the government will continue to back its obligations while retaining the support of its citizens. Although public backing has withered in numerous foreign countries, the government of the United States has achieved an enviable record of broad public support among its citizens.

The federal government possesses the unique advantage of being able to issue money to meet its obligations. This, along with its broad taxing power, means that federal government general obligations subject investors to virtually no business risk. As mentioned in Chapter 1, U.S. Treasury securities are the standard against which all other investments are compared for safety.

There are other organizations besides the federal government that subject investors to little uncertainty of return because of uncertain costs and revenues. A firm engaged in numerous unrelated operations is less reliant upon a limited source of income and generally finds it easier to weather problems that develop in one particular segment of the business. On the other hand, a firm dependent on a single product or service is likely to suffer serious repercussions from a major problem such as labor unrest, changing consumer tastes, or a lengthy supply interruption.

Even firms that concentrate their efforts in a single endeavor can have widely varying degrees of business risk. Businesses involved in activities such as the production of durable goods or high-tech electronics often generate revenues and profits that are subject to wide swings. Businesses in emerging industries are much more likely to experience unforeseen events that may threaten their economic viability. At the same time, firms engaged in producing goods and services that are staples may not make a great deal of money, but they generally exhibit fairly stable profits. Both retail grocery chains and utilities operate in fairly stable environments.

The need for a diversified source of income is also important to government organizations where a broad economic base is desirable. Cities and states that rely on a limited number of industries to support their revenue requirements face the possibility that a downturn in one or two of those industries might cripple the government's ability to provide services and meet other obligations.

Cities overly dependent on military installations, tourism, or a single large employer subject those who, in one way or another, depend on the cities to significant amounts of business risk. Municipal employees may find themselves without employment, and investors holding debt guaranteed by the cities may find their interest payments delayed or omitted because the municipalities are unable to continue gathering adequate tax revenues.

Business risk tends to be reduced through the ownership of short-term investments. The sooner money is to be returned, the less time there is for conditions to change sufficiently to affect an investor's rate of return. For example, a business firm with a single major product is unlikely to experience a steep decline in the demand for that product in a short period of time. Likewise, a city or state is less likely to experience a deterioration in its economic base during a month or even a year than during several years or a decade.

For a business, the reduction in business risk over short periods may be more applicable to the firm's creditors than to its owners. Even the public's impression that the demand for a product is declining can have a major impact on the market value of a firm's ownership. This altered impression is of some consequence to creditors but not nearly to the same degree. A reduction in the market value of a business may occur well before the decline in demand makes itself felt in the form of reduced revenues. The tremendous importance of investors' perceptions when they place a market value on the ownership of a business and the sudden changes in these perceptions are major factors in making ownership so risky.

FINANCIAL RISK

Financial risk refers to an investor's uncertain rate of return because an organization may be unable to meet its financial obligations.

These obligations generally consist of interest and principal payments on borrowed funds. Investments in organizations that are
heavily in debt tend to subject their owners to greater uncertainty of
return because of financial risk.

The Cause of Financial Risk

Unlike other forms of risk that can result from numerous sources,
financial risk is caused by a single factor; incurring fixed financial
obligations. These obligations may result from a desire to acquire
more assets or from a need to obtain funds to meet current spending requirements. These obligations generally result from debt, although leases can be equally burdensome and produce financial
risk. The more money an organization owes relative to its size and
the higher the rate of interest that must be paid on the loans, the
more likely that interest and principal obligations will become a
problem for the organization and the more likely that the market
value of investments in the organization will fluctuate. Financial
risk is that simple. It applies equally to businesses and government
organizations.

The financial risk has become an increasing concern for many investors as individuals, businesses, and governments have relied more
and more on debt to finance both current consumption and the
acquisition of assets. Greater government debt tends to force interest rates higher for all borrowers and squeeze private borrowers out
of the credit markets. Higher corporate debt resulting from corporate restructurings, leveraged buyouts, and debt-financed expansions produces more volatile earnings and makes it increasingly
likely that individual businesses will be unable to make interest and
principal payments in a timely manner.

The single cause of financial risk doesn't mean that two organizations of equal size with the same amount of money borrowed are
subject to the same degree of this risk. The kinds of assets an organization owns and the types of products or services it produces
also play important roles in the organization's ability to service its
debt. However, for the same organization, the more money it owes
and the higher the rate it pays on its borrowings, the greater the
degree of financial risk.

Short-term borrowing is more risky than long-term debt of the same amount. There are two reasons for the greater risk. First, the interest rate on short-term debt is subject to change either during the term the loan is outstanding or if and when the loan is renewed. An organization using short-term borrowing on a medium- or long-term basis assumes the very real risk that the interest rate on the loan will rise, thereby increasing the burden of the debt. Second, if the organization needs to refinance the loan, there is no way of knowing for certain if either the existing lender or any other lender will be willing to provide the needed funds. If the borrowing organization's fortunes deteriorate significantly between the time the original loan is made and the time the refinancing is required, the possibility exists that no lender will be located.

Investments That Reduce Financial Risk

The surest way for an investor to reduce his or her exposure to financial risk is to invest in sure things or something akin to them: investments in the federal government or in organizations that owe little or no money. The less money an organization owes relative to the size of its revenues and assets, the lower the degree of financial risk to which it subjects investors. If a company has no debt and no long-term leases then investors in the company don't have to concern themselves about fixed financial obligations.

Although there is always at least some small amount of risk inherent in borrowing money, certain organizations are better able than others to service debt. For example, a business with stable and predictable revenues is less likely to run into difficulties in servicing debt than is a firm with widely fluctuating revenues. Utilities such as telephone companies and gas transmission firms are able to handle a greater proportion of debt financing than are firms in very cyclical industries such as the manufacture of toys and capital goods. Thus, another method of reducing the exposure to financial risk is to stick with companies and industries that have a history of stable and predictable cash flows.

The previous section discussed the fact that financial risk is reduced when investments are scheduled to return cash in a short period of time. For example, short-term debt obligations of an organization have less financial risk than long-term obligations of the same organization, simply because there is less time for financial difficulties to occur. Thus, purchasing bonds issued by Chrysler Corporation with a one-year maturity would subject an investor to less financial risk than purchasing the firm's 20-year bonds.

Another consideration relating to financial risk is the uncertainty created by an investor's borrowing in order to purchase investment assets. Regardless of the kinds of investments acquired, borrowing for investment purposes significantly increases the risk exposure of an individual. Debt incurred to acquire investments may actually prove doubly troublesome, because most investment borrowing is at a variable rate of interest tied to the broker call rate. Borrowing money at a variable rate to invest in an asset that itself has significant exposure to financial risk is pouring gasoline onto the fire.

LIQUIDITY RISK

Liquidity risk refers to an investor's uncertain return because of the potential difficulty in liquidating the asset. The more difficult an asset is to sell without having to offer a large price concession, the greater the degree of liquidity risk in owning the asset.

Liquidity includes both the ability to turn an asset into cash and to do so without being required to significantly reduce the price below its current level. Virtually anything can be sold at some price. However, if the price obtainable is very low compared to what should be received under normal circumstances, owning the asset entails considerable risk.

Liquidity risk is of particular concern when there is some reason to believe an asset may be sold on short notice. For example, if there is a realistic possibility that assets will have to be sold to pay for some event, say a medical emergency or casualty loss, liquidity becomes a very important investment consideration. On the other hand, if there is no real prospect that an asset will be liquidated for many years, liquidity risk is not a serious issue.

The Cause of Liquidity Risk

Liquidity risk is largely a function of having an inactive resale market for an asset. Without an active market, potential buyers and sellers have a difficult time obtaining information and entering into transactions. Lack of an active secondary market may result from the recent origin of the asset and insufficient time to develop adequate channels of communication that would permit buyers and sellers to reach one another. An inactive market may also result from few buyers and sellers being interested in the asset. If an investor is an avid collector of some unique asset, say oriental birdhouses, it will be difficult to locate buyers if there is a need to dispose of the collection. The birdhouses thus present the investor with significant liquidity risk. Likewise, a particular bond issue or preferred stock issue may have very little investor interest, so that an investor wishing to sell a position in the security would have to offer a rather large discount to sell the security.

As a rule, assets that are not identical, or standardized, tend to have less active and efficient secondary markets. This differentiation is frequently troublesome to investors who have purchased tangible assets. When assets are similar in type but different in many details that affect their value, trading becomes more risky, because it is difficult to determine value without having the asset examined. This individual differentiation applies to antique automobiles, diamonds, coins, stamps, real estate, and many other assets. There may be some attempt to reduce the varieties of a particular type of asset by developing a set of investment quality categories as is currently done with stamps and coins, but differences will nearly always continue to exist within each group.

The liquidity of an asset tends to decline as the cost of transferring ownership increases. The price bid for an asset is partially determined by costs that the buyer must incur to take possession. For example, if significant transfer fees are imposed on the buyer by some government agency or by the institution that effects the transfer, the potential buyers can be expected to reduce the price that is offered for the asset.

Another factor influencing the liquidity of an asset is the relative size of an investor's holdings. An asset generally considered to be quite liquid may present difficulties to an investor wishing to dispose of an unusually large position in a short time. Disposing of 1,000 shares of a stock is one thing, but trying to sell 100,000 shares may be something else entirely. An active secondary market may be able to support moderate transactions on a continuous basis but be unable to support very large transactions without having the price significantly altered.

Investments That Reduce Liquidity Risk

Investments with an active secondary market have the least liquidity risk. For example, securities listed on the national securities exchanges and on the National Market System of the over-the-counter market generally tend to be fairly liquid. These securities must normally generate at least a moderate amount of investor interest and trading to qualify for trading in either of these markets. The market for government securities is enormous, so there is virtually no liquidity risk from holding these securities.

Many issues of securities trade only infrequently, so significant price changes may take place with each transaction. Numerous issues of preferred stock and corporate bonds may go untraded for weeks or months at a time. Because of their inactivity, these securities are generally quoted by dealers with relatively large differences between the bid and ask prices. These inactive securities subject an investor to significant liquidity risk.

As a rule, short-term assets have a greater degree of liquidity than long-term assets. This isn't always the case but it is true for the majority of investments. Very short-term investments such as money-market funds, money-market accounts, and NOW accounts have no real liquidity risk and essentially are the same as cash. Even assets like Treasury bills with slightly longer maturities have minimal liquidity risk.

Financial assets such as stocks, bonds, and options, because of their standardization, tend to provide more liquidity than tangible assets such as real estate, precious metals, and collectibles. Because one share of General Motors common stock is identical to any other share of General Motors common stock, a secondary market for trading the security is relatively easy to establish. At the other extreme, it is not always easy or cheap to resell a diamond, a 1954 Mickey Mantle baseball card, or a gold nugget at what a seller may consider a fair price.

REINVESTMENT RISK

Reinvestment risk was discussed briefly in the prior chapter as an element of interest-rate risk. Because of its importance in an era of relatively volatile interest rates and because reinvestment risk is frequently considered as a separate component of investment risk, it is worthwhile to discuss this risk in more detail.

The Cause of Reinvestment Risk

Reinvestment risk refers to an investor's uncertainty concerning the return that will be earned on the reinvestment of funds from an existing investment. These funds may result from periodic cash payments made to the investor, or they may result from a return of an investment's principal. Unless the returns from an investment are used for consumption, cash flows must be reinvested at whatever rate of return exists at the time the reinvestment is made. Because there is no way of knowing in advance what the reinvestment rate will be, considerable reinvestment risk is involved in owning most investments.

One of the risks of purchasing a three-year certificate of deposit is not knowing the rate of return that will be available three years down the road when the certificate matures. The rate may be higher—an outcome that would benefit the certificate owner. On the other hand, the rate may be considerably lower than the rate earned during the three-year period, an occurrence that would penalize the certificate owner. An investor who purchases a certificate of deposit that promises an annual return of 10 percent will be an unhappy person upon discovering that rates on new certificates have declined to 6 percent when the first certificate matures. Of course, if an individual buys the certificate with the expectation that the principal amount will be required for some other purpose, the reinvestment rate will be of no consequence.

Reinvestment risk is a special concern for someone who invests to generate a stream of periodic income payments. A retiree who depends on investment income to pay for food and shelter would be hard hit if an investment is renewed at a substantially reduced rate of return. The same hardship would befall someone disabled and dependent on current investment income to support a major portion of his or her personal spending.

Even an investor who invests to achieve long-term goals must be concerned with reinvestment risk. For example, a risk-averse investor may attempt to meet a retirement goal by limiting investments to low-risk, short-term assets. Cash flows are then reinvested as principal is returned in succeeding periods of short duration. Here the reinvestment risk stems from the possibility that rates may fall so that the investor is unable to earn a high enough return to achieve the goal.

Investments That Reduce Reinvestment Risk

Reinvestment risk is reduced with investments that do not pay out a large portion of their return currently and with investments that do not return principal for an extended period. The simple fact is that if there is no cash flow to reinvest, there is no reinvestment risk. If cash flows cannot be eliminated, then they should be minimized.

The greater the proportion of return that originates from an increase in value as opposed to current income, the less the reinvestment risk from owning the asset. An investment of any maturity has reinvestment risk if cash payments occur during the holding period. For example, a long-term certificate of deposit will subject its owner to reinvestment risk if the buyer chooses to have periodic interest paid in cash rather than reinvested in the certificate. On the other hand, if interest is automatically reinvested, the reinvested interest payments will earn whatever rate the certificate pays on the original principal so that the uncertainty concerning the return that these payments will earn is eliminated.

Exhibit 3–1 illustrates the increase in value at three different rates of reinvestment over a long period of time. The example assumes an original investment of $10,000 that guarantees an annual return of 9 percent with interest payments distributed monthly. Each $75 cash payment (one twelfth of the $900 in annual interest earned) is reinvested at either 6 percent, 9 percent, or 12 percent. Although the original principal continues to earn the original 9 percent return, the ability to reinvest interest payments at an annual rate of 12

Figure 3–1
Importance of the Reinvestment Rate

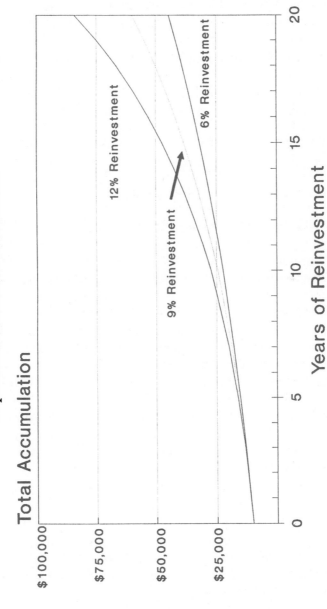

Total Accumulation

$100,000

$75,000

$50,000

$25,000

12% Reinvestment

9% Reinvestment

6% Reinvestment

0   5   10   15   20

Years of Reinvestment

$10,000 initial investment @ 9% with
cash distributed monthly

percent (compounded monthly) produces a final accumulation of $84,194 compared to $60,092 that would result from reinvesting interest at an annual rate of 9 percent. If the reinvestment rate is 6 percent the investor will accumulate only $44,653. The accumulation from a reinvestment rate of 9 percent is identical to the amount that would accumulate if the investor had chosen to have all of the cash distributions automatically reinvested into the certificate.

Reinvestment risk from security ownership can be reduced by acquiring securities that offer the largest proportion of expected returns in the form of price increases as opposed to current income. This includes low-coupon bonds selling at a discount from par and common stocks paying nominal dividends. The idea in each case is to choose securities in which there is the least amount of cash to reinvest.

By and large, tangible investments are owned for potential appreciation in value rather than current income, so the reinvestment risk from these assets is low. In this category of assets, real estate tends to generate the greatest amount of cash flow. For example, income property such as an office complex or rental housing will be expected to produce monthly cash flows that need to be reinvested. However, it is possible to reduce reinvestment risk by limiting investments to items such as property being held for development that normally makes little or no cash payments.

Reinvestment risk can be reduced by selecting investments with long maturities. For example, 30-year bonds have less reinvestment risk than five-year certificates of deposit which, in turn, have less reinvestment risk that one-year certificates of deposit. The longer the period of time a rate of return can be guaranteed, the less the reinvestment risk to which an investor is subjected.

MARKET RISK

Market risk is the uncertainy of return caused by market cycles, sudden market movements, and changes in public fashions among investment alternatives. Although market risk is unique in that the uncertain return applies to a particular investment or class of investments, it is a risk caused by factors that have little to do with the fundamentals of the investment.

The Causes of Market Risk

Market risk is more a matter of investor psychology than it is of financial analysis. Every dog has its day and every investment has a temporary, if recurring, window when investors sing its praises. The praises sometimes begin with a bang and sometimes with only a slow crawl that gradually gains momentum. Regardless of how it begins, however, the result is almost always the same; the entire process, hype and all, collapses from its own weight. The cycle has at one time or another affected virtually every type of investment. It has occurred with silver, real estate, nursing home stocks, growth stocks, gold, tulip bulbs, Florida real estate, and even good old buy-'em-and-hold-'em blue-chip stocks. It comes and it goes, and nobody is able to consistently predict what it will affect, when it will start, and how long it will last. The only certain thing is that the cycles will start and will run their course.

Market risk is especially important to investors who may need to liquidate an investment on relatively short notice. The risk is that the liquidation may occur during a down portion of the investment cycle. Thus, someone who needed to raise funds by selling stock late in the fourth quarter of 1987 was trapped by the sudden and unexpected stock market decline of October's Meltdown Monday. After the fact, when the shock had begun to wear off, a host of advisors, writers, and tardy prognosticators were quick to rationalize that stocks had been overpriced and were due for a major correction that would bring them to a more realistic valuation. In fact, virtually no one forecast the decline and its severity.

An even more pronounced decline took place in the silver market earlier in the decade. Following a spectacular price rise in silver to near $50 per ounce, the market plunged back into the single digits following government intervention in a scheme that purportedly would have allowed a few people to control the market for the metal. Regardless of the cause, the temporary runup and subsequent crash was only an exaggeration of the cycles that have occurred periodically with many other tangible and financial investments.

An investor who acquires an asset as a long-term investment holding with only the remotest possibility that the asset will have to be sold on short notice, has much less to worry about with respect to market risk. Investors who purchase investments to meet long-term goals can afford to ride out market cycles in whatever asset they select. Thus, a young investor accumulating stocks as part of a retirement fund will tend to be less concerned about sudden changes in value than will someone investing to achieve a short-term goal and who expects to cash in the investments in a matter of a few months or a few years.

Investments That Reduce Market Risk

Market risk is concentrated in investments of relatively long duration. Thus, short-term investments such as Treasury bills, certificates of deposit, money-market funds, and savings accounts have virtually no market risk. These investments return an investor's principal in such a short period that there is not time enough for a market cycle to occur. Even though investor interest in these very secure short-term instruments has its own ebbs and flows, shifts in interest do not affect the market value of the investments.

Among long-term investments, those that provide owners with large cash flows tend to have a reduced amount of market risk. Short of total disaster, investments such as high-grade government and corporate bonds, income stocks, preferred stocks, and income-producing property continue to provide cash flows for period after period regardless of what happens with respect to fads and market conditions. Because a large portion of the return from these investments is in current cash distributions, there will generally be considerably less valuation change from market fluctuations compared to investments expected to provide the majority of their return from price appreciation. Thus, the common stock of an electric utility will have a lower degree of market risk than the common stock of a high-tech computer concern. Likewise, a firm's bonds can be expected to have less market risk than the common stock of the same company.

Even among seemingly similar investments, the degree of market risk can be quite disparate. Some industries seem to be subject to continuous shifts of changing consumer sentiment that send common stocks of firms within the industries through violent price changes. These firms and industries are usually relatively young with uncertain prospects that can be subject to sudden change. On the other hand, more mature industries such as aluminum, automobile manufacturing, retailing, and branded-goods manufacturing are generally less severely affected by these changes in investment prospects. This doesn't mean that the securities of these firms are not subject to market risk; it just suggests that the cycles that cause market risk are not so severe and do not occur as frequently as they do with some other industries.

HOW INVESTMENT RISKS INTERACT

It is challenging enough that investors must concern themselves with identifying all of the individual risks applicable to the tremendous variety of investments available for purchase. A second and equally important aspect of risk analysis (one which muddies the investment waters even further) is how risks frequently interact with one another and how the interaction affects rates of return.

Some types of risk tend to operate independently of other risks, so that analyzing the effect of the uncertainties on an investment's rate of return is a relatively straightforward matter. For example, liquidity risk is an uncertainty unique even to different investments of the same general type. Many issues of bonds subject investors to significant amounts of liquidity risk, while other bonds can be sold quite easily.

Other risks act in concert to affect the rates of return on certain investments. The collective force of these risks acting together frequently produces a different result than would be expected on the basis of a single risk. Suppose two risks tend to simultaneously affect the rate of return on a particular investment. If the risks influence the investment's return in a similar manner (i.e., in either a positive manner or a negative manner) then the two risks reinforce one another and increase the volatility of the investment's return. On the other hand, if two risks affect an investment's return in an opposing manner (i.e., one in a positive manner and the other in a negative manner) the net result is that one tends to cancel the other. Even though one risk may have significantly greater influence, the net effect on an investment's return will be a reduced amount of uncertainty compared to when risks are unrelated or, especially, when they are positively related.

As an example of risk interaction, consider the positive relation-ship between inflation and interest-rate changes. With virtually all investments being influenced by both risks, the interaction between the two becomes an important consideration for any investor. The two risks reinforce one another to produce exaggerated changes in the return of some investments. For other investments the two risks tend to produce opposing forces.

For a long-term bond, higher inflation reduces the purchasing power of anticipated cash payments at the same time that rising interest rates drive down the bond's market value. Thus, these two risks that make themselves felt at the same time have the net effect of reinforcing changes in the return from owning long-term bonds. The interaction of risks makes life more uncertain for the unfor-tunate bondholder.

Alternatively, for investment vehicles that have historically benefited from inflation, the negative effects of higher interest rates (a higher return being demanded by investors) are at least partially canceled by the effects of higher inflation. Consider the case of a business engaged in mining precious metals, commodities with market prices that are positively influenced by rising inflationary expectations. At the same time that rising inflation reduces purchas-ing power, it tends to increase income and dividends, thereby producing a real income stream that could actually be increasing in real purchasing power.

While inflation by itself is likely to have a positive net effect for an owner of the mining company, rising interest rates have the effect of penalizing the value of ownership by increasing the return demanded of all investments including the mining of precious me-tals. Overall, it is possible that the net positive effect of rising infla-tion could overcome the negative effects of rising interest rates, so that the value of the mining concern actually increases. It is pos-sible, but certainly not a sure thing. Uncertainty surrounding the severity of the effects of individual risks and how they apply to the huge variety of investments is what makes evaluating the interac-tion of risks so difficult.

The bottom line is that when two risks interact to cancel the effects of one another for a particular investment, then the overall risk exposure to investors holding that investment is reduced. On the other hand, if two risks interact to amplify the effects of one another, then the overall risk exposure in owning that investment is increased.

SELF-HELP QUESTIONS

1. If the economy entered a sustained economic downturn, how would your investments be affected? Do you feel that you own any assets in which you could lose a substantial portion of the investment's principal?

2. How secure are the interest and dividend-paying capacities of your current investments? Would an economic downturn result in a likely reduction in any of your investment income? Could you live without a portion of this income?

3. Do the companies or organizations in which you have invested owe substantial amounts of money? Are the credit ratings satisfactory to suit your investment philosophy?

4. If interest rates declined substantially from current levels what would happen to your current investment income (not including the market value of the assets)?

5. In your own case, are you more concerned about a steady stream of investment income or a relatively steady investment value? Do the investment assets you own meet this investment philosophy?

6. Which of your investment assets are most affected by market cycles? Do you own any assets that are not at all affected by market risk? What have you given up in order to protect yourself against market risk?

7. If you had to sell each of your current investment assets, which ones would be most difficult to dispose of at a "fair" price? Which ones would be easiest to dispose of? Do you

think you have enough invested in liquid assets so that new investments can be acquired without concern about their liquidity?

Chapter
Four

THE RISKS OF
OWNING BONDS AND
PREFERRED STOCKS

It was not many years ago that fixed-income financial assets were a relatively homogeneous group of investments. These assets made a predetermined number of fixed payments and then returned the investor's principal. Thus, an investor bought $5,000 worth of bonds that promised to pay $200 every six months for 15 years, at which time the $5,000 was returned. This was indeed a simpler time.

In recent years investment bankers have used their extensive imaginations to create variations of fixed-income assets that appeal to every segment of the investment community. The added "bells and whistles" have produced assets that are difficult for investors to understand and challenging for brokers to explain. There are bonds that are convertible to silver, debentures that are convertible to cash, preferred stock that pays dividends in more shares of stock, and certificates from government-sponsored agencies that allow individual investors to collect mortgage principal and interest payments.

Despite all of these new wrinkles, most fixed-income securities have in common some basic elements. As a result, the majority of these assets subject investors to the same basic risks. Certain events tend to have a very strong influence on returns that investors earn from owning bonds and preferred stocks. Other uncertainties play a nominal role in affecting the returns on these securities.

CHARACTERISTICS OF FIXED-INCOME SECURITIES

A fixed-income security entitles its holder to a series of equal payments for a predetermined period of time. The size and frequency of the payments are set at the time the security is issued. The size, safety, and length of time that fixed-dollar payments are to be paid are the three overriding elements that influence the market value and the return on these investments. Most fixed-income investments return a designated lump sum of money at the end of the series of payments.

Examples of fixed-income financial assets abound. Hundreds of billions of dollars worth of bonds and notes are issued yearly by the federal government, foreign governments, municipalities, states, and business firms. The 1980s saw corporations issue huge amounts of new debt as a result of takeovers and leveraged buyouts. Preferred stock trails far behind corporate debt in relative importance but new issues of this hybrid security continue to come to market.

Many variations have developed on this theme of fixed payments. A small number of fixed-income debt securities have no maturity and are scheduled to make a series of payments forever. These "consols" or "perpetuities" have never been popular in the United States, although they have been issued in other countries. Preferred stock is a security that has no maturity. A limited number of fixed-income securities make a final payment that is based on some other variable. For example, a bond may make a final principal payment, the size of which is determined by the current market value of a prescribed number of ounces of silver. A more common variation is a fixed-income security that permits an investor to exchange the security for another asset.

Chapter 3 showed that some fixed-income assets automatically reinvest periodic income payments at the same rate of return being paid on the original principal. This systematic reinvestment replaces the actual payment of cash that would normally be made to the investor, and it significantly alters some of the risk aspects of the asset. One new breed of bond makes no cash-interest payments, but rather reinvests the scheduled interest. Automatic reinvestment results in the investor receiving at maturity a sum that includes all interest payments plus the interest earned on those payments. The downside is that it is necessary for the investor to wait a longer time before any money is received. No funds are available for spending or reinvestment until the investment is liquidated or until the issuer makes the final giant payment.

An investment that has gained great popularity in recent years is the mortgage-backed security, an investment that was originated to channel money into the real estate industry. This investment originates with government agencies such as the Government National Mortgage Association (Ginnie Maes) and the Federal Home Loan Mortgage Corporation (Freddie Mac) and with the Federal National Mortgage Association (Fannie Mae) and with private lending institutions. These certificates are sold to investors who then receive the principal and interest payments made by borrowers. Because mortgage loans backing the certificates are at fixed interest rates, the market values of the certificates behave much like regular bonds.

It is impossible to analyze every variation of the fixed-income financial assets available for purchase. The discussion in this chapter will primarily center on the "plain vanilla" version of these securities—those that make fixed payments for a stated period. This includes the vast majority of bonds and preferred-stock issues.

Alterations to these basic elements are likely to affect one or more of the risks that apply to the standard model. For example, a bond that is convertible into shares of common stock reduces some of the risks applicable to regular bonds at the same time that it entails new risks normally not a concern to bondholders. Likewise, mortgage-backed securities, because they return a portion of principal with each payment, tend to produce risks that are similar but not exactly the same as those facing ordinary bondholders.

PURCHASING-POWER RISK

The loss of purchasing power caused by unexpected inflation is one of the most serious risks facing the owners of fixed-income securities. Unexpected inflation affects virtually all fixed-income securities and can severely diminish an investor's ability to acquire goods and services with investment cash flow. The effects of purchasing-power risk are so widespread and can be so devastating that unless an issuer is in such poor financial condition that considerable doubt exists that payments will be made at all, inflation is probably the single greatest risk investors in fixed-income securities must assume.

Inflation and the Decline in Real Purchasing Power

Because fixed-income securities are scheduled to make a series of constant payments, inflation will make each successive payment worth less in terms of the goods and services that can be purchased. Depending on the number of years the investor plans to hold the security and the rate of inflation during the holding period, payments scheduled to occur many years in the future may be nearly devoid of purchasing power.

The effect of various rates of inflation on purchasing power for selected time intervals is displayed in Exhibit 4–1. The chart assumes that an investor purchases a $1,000 principal-amount bond with a 25-year maturity. If inflation averages 7 percent annually during the entire 25 years, the final $1,000 repayment of principal will have purchasing power of only $184 measured in terms of prices that existed when the bond was purchased. Thus, the dollars invested in the bond will have lost nearly 82 percent of their purchasing power when the principal is finally returned. Even a relatively moderate 5-percent inflation will reduce the purchasing power of the original $1,000 investment to $295 when the loan is repaid.

At the same time that inflation plays havoc with the real value of a bond's principal, it causes progressive deterioration in the purchasing power of fixed-interest payments. Within the series, the longer the time before an individual payment is to be received, the less it is worth in terms of what can be purchased. Even moderate

Exhibit 4–1
Inflation and the Real Value of $1,000

Annual Rate of Inflation (%)	Years Until $1,000 is Received				
	5	10	15	20	25
4	$822	$676	$555	$456	$375
5	784	614	481	377	295
6	747	558	417	312	233
7	713	508	362	258	184
10	621	386	239	149	92
15	497	247	123	61	30

inflation reduces the value of the interest payment to be received in the tenth year of a 20-year bond compared to the interest payment received in the first year.

To demonstrate the declining purchasing power of a stream of interest payments, assume an investor purchases a $1,000 par, 10-percent coupon bond with a 15-year maturity. Depending on the rate of inflation during the ensuing holding period, the real purchasing power of each of the interest payments and the final repayment of the principal are illustrated in Exhibit 4–2. The relatively large sum in year 15 includes the purchasing power of both the final $100 interest payment and the return of the $1,000 principal.

The real purchasing power of all the bond's payments including the return of principal totals exactly $1,000 when the rate of inflation averages 10 percent annually (i.e., adding all of the dollar amounts in the 10-percent column). In other words, earning an annual return of 10 percent when prices are increasing at an annual rate of 10 percent leaves the investor in exactly the same position in terms of real purchasing power. The only change is that the purchasing power of the original $1,000 investment is spread over the years that the payments are received. At an inflation rate higher than the return earned, the real value of the total payments to be

Exhibit 4–2
Real Purchasing Power of Bond Payments
(15-year, 10%-coupon, $1,000 par)

Year of Payment	Rate of Inflation (%)					
	0	3	5	7	10	15
1	100	94	91	87	83	76
2	100	94	91	87	83	76
3	100	92	86	82	75	66
4	100	89	82	76	68	57
5	100	86	78	71	62	50
6	100	84	75	67	56	43
7	100	81	71	62	51	38
8	100	79	68	58	47	33
9	100	77	64	54	42	28
10	100	74	61	51	39	25
11	100	72	58	48	35	21
12	100	70	56	44	32	19
13	100	68	53	41	29	16
14	100	66	51	39	26	14
15	1,100	706	529	398	263	135

received will amount to less than the original investment. Conversely, if the return on the investment is greater than the rate of inflation during the holding period, there will be an increase in the real purchasing power of the investor's funds.

If taxes are due on the interest payments or on any gain realized when the bond matures or is sold, an investor must earn a before-tax return higher than the inflation rate to keep purchasing power from being depleted. For example, an investor in a 25 percent marginal tax bracket (i.e., paying income taxes at a rate of 25-percent of extra income) has an after-tax return of only 7.5 percent from a bond that yields 10 percent. Annual inflation of more than 7.5 percent results in the investor losing purchasing power.

Expected and Unexpected Inflation

Chapter 1 explained that inflation anticipated by investors is embodied in the rates of return investments are expected to pay. Because investors in fixed-income investments are compensated for expected inflation in the rates of return they earn, the possibility of unexpected inflation is the real cause of the purchasing-power risk that these individuals face. For example, a bond with a 10-percent yield promises a real return of 3 percent if inflation is expected to average 7 percent. The 10-percent yield exists only because investors expect 7-percent inflation and have built it into the pricing of the bond.

If inflation turns out to be considerably worse than expected, the real rate of return will be less than expected and may actually prove to be negative. Should inflation average less than expected over the life of the investment, the investor benefits from a higher real rate of return compared to the return anticipated at the time the investment was purchased. In each case it is the unexpected inflation or lack of it that produces the uncertainty in the investor's rate of return, and it is unexpected inflation that causes purchasing-power risk.

In summary, bonds and preferred stock subject investors to considerable uncertainty of return because of purchasing-power risk. The longer the time before an investment's principal is returned, the greater the degree of uncertainty. Keeping in mind that assets are priced to compensate investors for anticipated changes in consumer prices, it is deviations from expected inflation that prove to be the significant threat that must be considered in the selection of an investment.

INTEREST-RATE RISK

The likelihood that interest rates will change subjects investors to substantial uncertainty regarding the return that will be earned by bonds and preferred stock. The negative relationship between movements in interest rates and the market value of a fixed-income investment means that rising interest rates will reduce the market value of fixed-income investments such as bonds and preferred stocks. Because of this relationship, there is considerable uncertainty about the price one of these investments will bring if it should become necessary to sell the asset in the secondary market prior to its scheduled maturity.

Even an investor who intends to hold a fixed-income asset until maturity stands to lose, if only indirectly, when interest rates rise. The decrease in value may not seem to concern a long-term investor, but the fact is that the owner of the security could have been earning a higher return. In addition, even long-term investors sometimes discover that they unexpectedly need to liquidate assets on short notice. Should this occur, fixed-income securities may have to be sold at a loss if there are insufficient short-term assets in the investor's portfolio.

The Importance of Maturity Length

The uncertain return from a fixed-income asset because of interest-rate changes is directly related to the length of time before the asset matures. A long maturity means that an asset will exhibit large swings in market value when interest rates change. Thus, owners of long-term bonds and preferred stocks suffer more interest-rate risk than do owners who hold shorter maturities that go through only minor price swings as interest rates change.

Exhibit 4–3 illustrates the market prices of two bonds with different maturity lengths in various interest-rate environments. One bond has 15 years remaining until the $1,000 principal is to be repaid, while the second bond has only two years remaining before it matures with the same $1,000 value. Both bonds have the same 10-percent coupon rate.

Each bond sells at its par value when the market rate of interest is 10 percent, the same as the coupon rate. A 10-percent coupon bond of any maturity sells at par in a market that demands 10 percent from investments of comparable risk. When the market rate of interest rises, the price of the long-term bond falls considerably more than does the price of the short-term bond. An increase in the market rate of interest to 14 percent results in a market price of $751 for the 15-year bond and a market price of $932 for the short-term bond. Thus, from an original price of $1,000, an increase in the

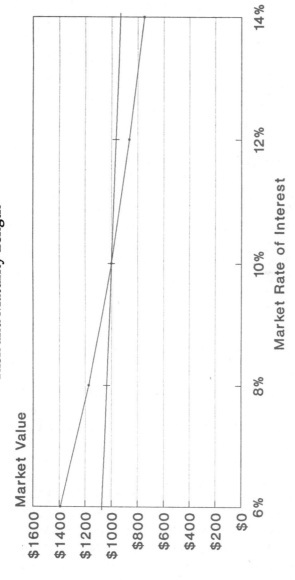

Exhibit 4–3
Risk and Maturity Length

Market Value

$1600

$1400

$1200

$1000

$800

$600

$400

$200

$0

6%   8%   10%   12%   14%

Market Rate of Interest

──── 15–Year Maturity   ──+── 2–Year Maturity

10% Coupon Bonds

market rate of interest from 10 percent to 14 percent causes the long-term bond to lose nearly 25 percent of its market value, while the short-term bond loses only 7 percent of its market value.

While the long-term bond is subject to greater price declines from interest-rate increases, it also experiences significantly greater increases in price when market interest rates decline. For example, a decrease in interest rates from 10 percent to 6 percent results in a $372 increase in the price of the 15-year bond to $1,372, while the short-term bond rises by only $72 to $1,072.

This example clearly illustrates that a long-term bond has the potential of producing much bigger gains and losses because of changes in market rates of interest. This potential for major changes is not necessarily bad. If an investor is expecting a major decline in interest rates, a long-term bond is likely to be the asset of choice. However, in terms of interest-rate risk, uncertain returns are directly related to the maturity length of a fixed-income investment. The longer the maturity, the greater the price swings from interest-rate movements. The greater the price swings, the greater the uncertainty of an investment's rate of return.

The Importance of Coupon Size

Another important determinant of interest-rate risk is the size of a security's interest or dividend coupon. The larger the coupon, the greater the proportion of total return that originates from periodic cash payments that occur evenly throughout the life of the security. The earlier cash is returned to investors, the less the market value of the security is influenced by interest-rate changes.

A high-coupon bond is subject to smaller price swings when interest rates change than is a low-coupon bond with the same maturity date and yield to maturity. The earlier return of cash from the high-coupon bond permits an investor to reinvest the cash payments at the current rate of interest, so that higher market rates of interest do not impose as great a penalty. On the other hand, low-coupon bonds provide a greater proportion of an investor's return from the repayment of principal, which may not occur for many years. The longer time until receipt of such a large part of the cash flow means that interest-rate changes will produce major swings in the market price of the security.

Mortgage-backed securities tend to subject investors to less interest-rate risk than do ordinary bonds, because the former return a portion of principal as well as interest each period. Thus, if interest rates rise, the owner of a Ginne Mae will be able to reinvest interest and part of the principal.

The security with the greatest price variability caused by interest-rate changes pays its entire return in one lump sum at a specified future date. For example, a zero-coupon bond makes no periodic interest payments to the investor but, rather, automatically reinvests interest to increase what is called the "accreted" value of the bond. This reinvested interest cannot be obtained from the issuer until the bond matures. Zero-coupon bonds are subject to very large adjustments in market value when interest rates change, because the owner has no opportunity to reinvest any cash payments prior to maturity. Thus, if market interest rates rise, the investor is unable to get any cash from the bond that can be reinvested at the new, higher rate. On the positive side, if market rates of interest fall, the investor need not worry about investing cash flows at an interest rate lower than the return promised by the bond's issuer.

Exhibit 4–4 illustrates the price movements for three 25-year maturity bonds with different coupon rates when the market rate of interest moves from 8 percent to 12 percent. Then the market rate of interest is 8 percent, the 12-percent coupon bond will sell for $1,430, the 6-percent coupon bond will sell for $785, and the zero-coupon bond will sell for $141. If the market rate of interest climbs to 12 percent, the same bonds will fall to prices of $1,000, $527, and $54, respectively. In percentage terms, the declines are 30 percent for the 12-percent coupon bond, 33 percent for the 6-percent coupon bond, and 62 percent for the zero-coupon bond. Thus, the lower the coupon rate on a bond, the more sensitive its market value will be to changes in the market rate of interest.

Duration

Duration uses both a bond's maturity length and coupon in a numerical measure of interest-rate risk. In general, the longer the

Exhibit 4-4
Risk and Cash Flow

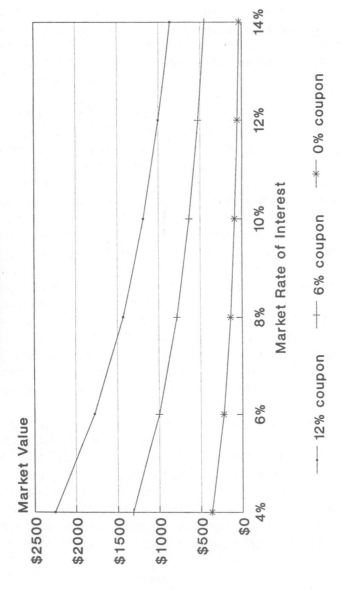

Market Value

$2500

$2000

$1500

$1000

$500

$0

4%   6%   8%   10%   12%   14%

Market Rate of Interest

—•— 12% coupon   —+— 6% coupon   —*— 0% coupon

25-year Bonds

maturity and the lower the coupon rate, the larger the duration and the greater the interest-rate risk from owning the investment. The investment with the greatest interest-rate risk is the zero-coupon bond for which duration is equal to the number of years to maturity. For a bond that provides cash flows prior to maturity (i.e., any bond with current interest payments), the duration will be less than the number of years to maturity. A more detailed discussion, along with the relatively complicated methodology for calculating duration, is in Appendix A.

FINANCIAL RISK

The degree of financial risk associated with fixed-income securities spans a wide range. At the low end of this range are securities issued and guaranteed by the United States government. These investments are essentially free of financial risk regardless of their maturity length. At the opposite end of the scale are fixed-income securities issued by highly leveraged projects or organizations. Low-rated debt securities that qualify as "junk" bonds are examples of fixed-income securities that subject owners to large financial risk. Some of the riskiest of these bonds have uncertainty of how many interest payments will be made, let alone whether principal will ever be returned.

Identifying Financial Risk

The degree of financial risk from owning a particular fixed-income security can be identified fairly easily. For example, a bond or preferred stock issued by an organization that uses very little borrowed money subjects an investor to minimal financial risk. On the other hand, fixed-income securities issued by organizations with heavy debt burdens subject investors to great uncertainty as to whether the organization will be able to meet its financial commitments. An organization's reliance on debt financing is certainly not a foolproof method of viewing financial risk, but it is often a good indicator of how the organization's management feels about using borrowed funds.

Financial risk varies not only with the degree to which debt is used but also with an organization's ability to handle the debt. For example, many regulated businesses such as electric utilities and water companies are able to use borrowed funds for a relatively large proportion of their capital needs and still service their financial obligations without great strain. These firms tend to have relatively secure and predictable cash flows to service preferred-stock dividends and interest and principal payments on debt. Other businesses with cash patterns that are more difficult to forecast find that even a relatively small amount of borrowing may create financial difficulties. Thus, financial risk is a function not only the extent to which an organization uses fixed-cost financing in its capital structure, but also the ability of the organization to service the fixed obligations.

The financial risk inherent in owning a fixed-income asset can change after an investment has been acquired. A firm's management may decide to undertake a recapitalization and issue additional fixed-cost securities to raise funds to retire shares of common stock. The change in financing mix may be designed to improve the firm's stock price or to make it more difficult for a corporate raider to acquire control of the firm. In the latter-1980s the leveraged buyout (LBO) became a frequent news item as management groups bought out stockholders with borrowed funds. These LBOs made existing bondholders unhappy as they watched their own financial risk shoot upward overnight.

The degree of financial risk for fixed-income investors may change more gradually as a firm expands its asset base through debt financing. For example, a firm's management may feel that increased debt will increase shareholder value by increasing the return the firm is able to earn on its equity. This policy may indeed benefit the company's common stockholders, but at the same time it is likely to prove harmful to the holders of the firm's debt and preferred stock, thereby reducing the value of their investments.

Long-term, fixed-income investments tend to subject their owners to greater amounts of uncertainty from financial risk, simply because it is not possible for an investor to know what the future holds 15 to 20 years down the road. A fixed-income investment that currently appears to subject its owners to very little financial risk may turn out to have an entirely different appearance in another 10 years. Most investors who purchased long-term bonds of giant corporations 10 or 15 years ago had no idea that some of these firms would be taken private or merged into other organizations.

Occasional investors are normally unable to evaluate all of the factors that influence financial risk. If there was only a single crucial financial ratio, say the proportion of assets financed by debt, then there could be some standard that would indicate that an investment was "moderate" or "average" with respect to financial risk. Unfortunately, too many factors influence financial risk for a single ratio to have such powers.

Financial Risk and the Rating Agencies

Although no magic ratio exists, there are independently derived and publicly available ratings of financial risk for many fixed-income investments. Actually, the ratings indicate more than just financial risk, but they are good indicators of an organization's ability to service individual issues of its fixed-income obligations. The fact that this independent measure is readily available greatly simplifies an investor's task in analyzing investments for financial risk.

Standard & Poor's and Moody's are the two major financial services offering ratings for fixed-income investments. Each organization grades hundreds of investments on a scale that ranges from very low risk, or investment grade, to very high risk, or speculative grade. Investments judged to have an unusually low degree of risk carry AAA ratings, while investments with a very high degree of risk carry ratings in the Cs. The lowest rating considered to be investment grade by Standard & Poor's is BBB. A similar grading by Moody's is Baa.

Ratings of fixed-income investments are available in either *Moody's Bond Record* or Standard & Poor's *Bond Guide*. Most public and college libraries carry one or both of these monthly publications in the reference section. The rating agencies continually review organizations' ability to service their obligations. As this ability changes, the rating for a particular fixed-income security may be upgraded or downgraded. A detailed breakdown of the grading categories for fixed-income investments along with information on how these gradings are determined is in Appendix B.

BUSINESS RISK

The uncertain returns caused by business risk are less for fixed-income investors than for owners of equities. U.S. government securities such as Treasury bonds and Ginnie Mae mortgage-backed securities subject an investor to virtually no uncertainty from this risk. At the same time, fixed-income investments secured by the unstable revenues of a company operating in a cyclical industry may subject investors to significant uncertainty regarding their own payments.

The Causes of Business Risk

Business risk for owners of bonds and preferred stocks stems from the uncertainty of an organization's revenues and costs. Uncertain cash flows caused by unstable or deteriorating economic conditions plague most organizations. A deteriorating economic environment is damaging to political entities (i.e., Brazil, Louisiana, and many towns in the Southwest United States) as well as to virtually any type of business. Likewise, the expenses that must be borne by an organization are not always stable or predictable. Undependable revenues and costs make the viability of organizations uncertain. This uncertainty is harmful to the owners of fixed-income securities because it makes the repayment of interest, dividends, and principal less certain. Thus, except for special types of investments such as those insured by stable national governments, investments nearly always subject investors to a certain amount of business risk.

In general, fixed-income securities with short maturities carry considerably less business risk than investments with longer maturities. A five-year bond has less uncertainty of return from business risk than does a 25-year bond of the same organization, because there is less time for revenues and costs to deteriorate. The revenues of government organizations and businesses generally decline gradually over time rather than all at once.

Business risk depends heavily on the source of an organization's revenues. The more diversified the sources of revenue, the more likely that payments to fixed-income investors will occur as scheduled. Thus, governments with a highly diversified economic base and businesses involved in producing or selling a number of unrelated products or services are better able to weather the business downturns that occur in specialized segments of the economy. On the other hand, organizations that put all of their eggs into one basket may find themselves unable to meet their obligations.

How Business Risk Varies by Type of Investment

The uncertainty of return caused by business risk varies with the type of fixed-income security owned. Some fixed-income investments, generally those with a lesser claim on the issuer, subject their owners to greater uncertainty of return. In comparing investments of the same organization, a higher priority claim means less business risk. For securities of the same company, debt subjects investors to less uncertainty than preferred stock, because payments to debt holders are legally required, while dividends to holders of preferred stock are voted on by the firm's directors.

Debt is not homogeneous with respect to business risk. Debt secured by specific assets subjects an investor to less uncertainty than debt of the same organization secured only by the issuer's promise to pay. Holders of secured debt have distinct assets to claim in the event the borrower fails to maintain timely payments on the obligations. In general, unsecured debt such as debentures and subordinated debentures can subject their holders to significant uncertainty because of business risk. If cash flows deteriorate or expenses rise to the point that an organization is forced into bankruptcy, a strong possibility exists that the owners of unsecured obligations will receive considerably less than the face value of their claims, and even these recoveries will occur after a prolonged period during which no interest payments will be made.

The degree of business risk embodied in a fixed-income security is partially reflected by the grading assigned to the investment by the rating agencies. Ratings reflect a great many variables, and one of the significant considerations is the uncertainty of an issuer's cash flows—both revenues and expenses. In general, the greater the uncertainty of cash flows, the lower the rating that is assigned to a particular investment.

The quality of the assets that collateralize a particular investment is also considered in the rating process. The more valuable and liquid the collateral backing a particular security, the higher the rating that is awarded. An issuer that has a relatively low overall credit rating can have a fixed-income security that has a higher rating if the collateral pledged against the obligation is sufficiently valuable and liquid.

LIQUIDITY RISK

Liquidity risk refers to the uncertainty of return that derives from the fact that a fixed-income security may be difficult to resell. The greater the likelihood that an investor may have difficulty in liquidating an asset, the greater the uncertainty concerning the rate of return that will be earned. Liquidity risk varies significantly among the various types of fixed-income securities.

Because the majority of investors are concerned about liquidity, fixed-income investments with limited liquidity generally offer slightly higher returns than similar investments that are very actively traded. For example, a long-term bond that is seldom traded will generally offer a higher yield than an active bond with the same maturity and other risk characteristics. Because of the difference in yields, investors willing to accept reduced liquidity can generally earn slightly higher returns by selecting assets with reduced liquidity.

Differences in Liquidity Among Fixed-Income Securities

Some fixed-income investments have an active secondary market and are easy to sell, so they subject investors to virtually no liquidity risk. Treasury securities of nearly any kind and many actively traded federal agency bonds and corporate bonds are easy to convert into cash without having to accept a low bid from a dealer or from another investor.

On the other hand, some fixed-income assets have a very limited secondary market. A great many issues of preferred stocks and corporate and municipal bonds trade infrequently, so investors who wish to sell these securities may discover a relatively large difference between the current bid and the price at which the last trade occurred.

Many bond and preferred stock issues are relatively small, so there are not many bonds or shares of stock in a particular issue to trade in the secondary market. In addition, a large portion of many fixed-income issues have been purchased by a few big institutional investors, which limits trading in the secondary market. Also, the issuer may have retired a large portion of the original issue. All of these events will result in reduced liquidity for individual issues of fixed-income securities.

Reducing Liquidity Risk

Investors can take certain precautions to minimize liquidity risk from fixed-income investments. In the case of corporate bonds, an investor can restrict purchases to bonds traded on the organized security exchanges, such as the American Stock Exchange or the New York Stock Exchange. A limited number of bonds are also traded on the regional exchanges. Listed corporate bonds are frequently more active than corporate bonds that trade in the over-the-counter market. Another advantage of listed corporates is that it is easier to obtain a price quotation, because the closing prices are carried in the financial pages of many daily newspapers.

Another method of minimizing liquidity risk is to stick with bonds that are part of large issues. Large, widely held bond issues tend to be more actively traded and offer an investor greater liquidity. For example, an investor might want to check on the size of a new issue of municipal bonds before entering a purchase order. Brokers should be able to inform an investor if a bond has or will have a significant secondary market.

Another way to keep from running into liquidity problems is to stick with fixed-income securities of a well-known issuer. This is perhaps more important in purchasing municipal bonds, because there are so many different borrowers, but it applies to the corporate market as well. Bonds of well-known issuers tend to trade better and offer more liquidity than the securities of little-known organizations.

REINVESTMENT RISK

Reinvestment risk for fixed-income investors relates to the uncertainty caused by not knowing the return at which cash flows from an investment can be reinvested. Thus, the owner of preferred stock or of an ordinary bond does not know in advance the rate at which the dividends or interest can be reinvested. The risk for fixed-income investors is that the rate at which flows can be reinvested will be lower than expected, thereby reducing the overall return on the investment.

Reinvestment risk can be a significant concern for owners of fixed-income investments, depending on an investor's personal needs and the types of investments owned. In general, fixed-income securities with short maturities subject owners to greater reinvestment risk, because interest as well as principal must be reinvested. Reinvestment risk is relatively large for Treasury bills and corporate-debt securities with short maturities. The risk is much lower for owners of preferred stocks and long-term bonds.

Chapter 3 discussed the importance of the proportion of an investment's return that derives from current cash flows in determining reinvestment risk. In general, the higher the proportion of total return represented by interest and dividend payments, the greater the reinvestment risk. A high-coupon bond continually spits out large amounts of cash that must be reinvested at whatever rate of return is available at the time the cash is received. On the other hand, a low-coupon bond that sells at a discount from par makes relatively small cash payments that need to be reinvested.

Mortgage-backed securities such as Ginnie Maes are subject to substantial reinvestment risk, because both interest and a portion of principal must be reinvested each period. Even more important to owners of these securities is the fact that when market interest rates fall, borrowers will begin refinancing loans and principal repayments will become much larger. Thus, at the very time when a fixed-income security with a high coupon appears to be a very good investment, borrowers will begin early repayment on the underlying loans. The Ginnie Mae owner will then be stuck with reinvesting these large cash flows at the lower market rates of interest.

The reinvestment risk for an investor owning a fixed-income security is substantially higher if a security is subject to being called by the issuer. A bond or preferred stock that is subject to being called prior to maturity results in an investor being unsure when funds will have to be reinvested. This uncertainty regarding when principal will be returned means that there will be great uncertainty concerning the return that will be earned on reinvested funds. When an investor knows the date that principal will be returned there is uncertainty as to the return that will be earned on reinvested funds. When the date of principal return is also uncertain, the problem of estimating the return on reinvested funds is compounded.

The ultimate in protection against reinvestment risk is provided by a zero-coupon bond with a long maturity. This security derives all of its return from scheduled increases in accreted value, so there is no cash to reinvest until the bond is called or reaches maturity. Such a tactic entails other serious risks, but for the investor mainly concerned about a reduced rate of return from cash-flow reinvestment, selecting zero-coupon bonds minimizes reinvestment risk.

MARKET RISK

Market risk refers to a fixed-income investor's uncertainty caused by market cycles and changes in investor preferences toward particular segments of the market. The greater the size and frequency of these changes, the more volatile the market value of the fixed-income security and the less certain the price at which the investment can be liquidated.

For example, investors may alter their preferences with regard to risk and move funds from low-rated to high-rated bonds. This movement of funds will cause low-rated bonds to decline in price relative to investment-grade bonds. At other times when investors are in an upbeat mood and less concerned with risk, they may move funds to low-rated bonds to obtain the higher expected returns these securities provide. This flow of money will result in an upward cycle for low-rated bonds with respect to the prices of high-rated bonds.

Although the degree of market risk can vary somewhat depending on the particular fixed-income asset being considered, investments with fixed payouts tend to be subject to smaller market cycles and, thus, have lesser amounts of market risk than do tangible assets or equity securities. At the same time, they subject investors to greater market risk than nonmarketable investments such as savings accounts and savings bonds.

SUMMARIZING RISK AND FIXED-INCOME INVESTMENTS

Like virtually all other investments, fixed-income assets have their share of risks that lurk for unsuspecting investors. Some of the risks are very important and can result in significant reductions in the real returns earned. Other risks are less important but still worthy of consideration.

Probably the single most important risk of owning fixed-income assets is the possibility of large reductions in purchasing power as a result of price inflation. Anyone who invests funds in an asset that makes fixed dollar payments over a long period of time takes a real risk that, by the time the payments are actually received, they will be worth very little in real terms. While an expected level of inflation is built into the rate of return an investment provides, unexpected inflation can prove to be a very destructive force for fixed-income investors, because there is no chance that payments will be altered to compensate for the inflation.

Another significant risk for owners of fixed-income securities is uncertainty with respect to future market rates of interest. Rising interest rates can significantly reduce the market values of existing fixed-income investments. For the majority of individual investors in fixed-income securities, interest-rate risk is probably less important than purchasing-power risk.

Both purchasing-power risk and interest-rate risk can best be reduced by selecting short-term, fixed-income securities. Short-term investments mature in such a brief time that it is highly unlikely that either inflation or higher interest rates will prove to be a real threat to the expected rate of return. The shorter the term of the investment, the less the uncertainty of return because of unexpected changes in inflation or interest rates.

Business risk and financial risk are best guarded against by sticking with securities issued or insured by the U.S. government. The latter category includes securities such as mortgage participations from Ginnie Mae. Outside of government-related investments, securities issued by financially strong industry leaders tend to subject their owners to small amounts of uncertainty from business and financial risks. Without scouring through massive amounts of unfathomable financial statements, investors can limit their exposure to these two risks by restricting their fixed-income holdings to securities rated highly by one or both of the major rating agencies. Fixed-income securities rated A, AA, and AAA indicate that modest amounts of both business and financial risk are involved in owning the securities.

Liquidity risk can be eliminated as a concern by avoiding fixed-income investments that have a very inactive secondary market or, in some cases, no secondary market at all. A multitude of fixed-income investments with very active resale markets are available, so there is no real reason for an investor to suffer from liquidity risk if this uncertainty is deemed important.

Reinvestment risk is minimized by limiting investments to preferred stocks and long-term bonds in which principal does not require reinvestment for many years. Bonds that offer most or all of their returns from gains in value rather than from periodic cash payments provide more protection against reinvestment risk than do securities that make large cash distribution in dividends or interest. Like liquidity risk, reinvestment risk is relatively easy to avoid by being selective in the choice of investments. On the other hand, if an investor intends to use the periodic payments for consumption rather than for reinvestment, reinvestment risk is not a threat and need not be considered in selecting an investment.

Market risk is not as great a concern for investors purchasing fixed-income securities as it is when they purchase other types of investments. This risk is caused by market cycles and can be avoided altogether by limiting fixed-income investments to assets with short maturities. If investments are to be held for a long time, then market risk is of limited importance.

Overall, it is fairly clear that fixed-income assets with short maturities significantly reduce most of the risks that can plague investors. The exception, and a risk that should not be overlooked, is the possibility that funds may have to be reinvested at a reduced rate of return. Even reinvestment risk is not an important concern for investors who plan to use cash payments and the principal for some purpose other than reinvestment.

A method of balancing the lower returns offered by short-term securities and the higher risks inherent in most long-term, fixed-income securities is to stagger, or ladder, maturities. Thus, rather than investing a great deal of money in bonds maturing in a single year or in several distant years, an investor can hedge by purchasing equal numbers of bonds maturing in consecutive years. As the short bonds reach maturity, funds can be reinvested in bonds of longer maturities that offer higher yields.

Laddering maturities permits an investor wishing to own fixed-income securities to avoid the most severe outcomes of nearly all types of risk, as long as the bonds purchased have been issued by a diverse group of organizations. The exception to this diversification is laddering U.S. Treasuries, which would subject an owner to virtually no business or financial risk. Diversification and coordinating securities with personal goals will be discussed in Chapter 8.

SELF-HELP QUESTIONS

1. Looking at your own investment portfolio, what proportion is composed of fixed-income assets with long maturities? If both inflation and interest rates rise above their current levels, to what extent will these assets be affected?

2. What portion of your current return on fixed-income assets is being eaten away by inflation? Do you feel that these assets are providing you with sufficient returns, given your own expectations regarding inflation over the next 5 to 10 years?

3. What considerations entered into acquiring the fixed-income securities that you currently own? Do you have the same concerns now as you did when you acquired these invest-

ments? When you acquired your current fixed-income investments, did you understand how their market values could be affected by interest rate changes?

4.   What degree of liquidity do your current fixed-income investments have? Do you foresee any time within the next five years when you may need to liquidate any of your long-term securities? Is there any reason to believe that there may be some difficulty in liquidating any of your fixed-income securities?

5.   If you had a choice between a one-year 15-percent certificate of deposit and a five-year 14-percent (annual rate) certificate of deposit, which would you select? If you chose the one-year certificate what would you do with the money when the certificate matured? What return could you expect on any reinvestment? If you chose the five-year certificate and needed the money after only one year, what penalty would be required to redeem the certificate?

6.   If the economy enters into an extended recession, what is the risk that some of the income you receive from fixed-income investments will be reduced?

7.   If you had a choice between an ultra-safe fixed-income investment that returned 9 percent annually over 10 years and another investment with the same maturity that offered an expected yield of 12 percent annually but with considerably more risk, which would you choose?

8.   If yields on short-term securities are higher than on securities of substantially longer maturity, which would you choose? Are there any risks in the course of action you have chosen?

Chapter
Five

THE RISKS OF OWNING COMMON STOCKS AND RELATED SECURITIES

Despite the risks inherent in common stock ownership and the traumatic shock of 1987's Meltdown Monday, common stocks remain a popular investment among both individual and institutional investors. One of the main reasons for this continuing popularity is the possibility of the "big score" from an ownership position in common stocks. While such a spectacular return may be unlikely (at least in the short-run), the possibility of riches is nearly always there. Takeovers, buyouts, big government contracts, and the investment community's sudden realization that a particular stock is grossly undervalued are prospects that lie just over the horizon.

CHARACTERISTICS OF COMMON STOCKS

A share of common stock represents an ownership claim on a corporation. Large corporations may have their ownership divided over many millions of shares of common stock, while smaller corporations may have shares of ownership that number only in the thousands or even hundreds. The more segments into which a corporation is divided, the less the claim and the lower the value of each individual piece. If Coca-Cola Company had 37 million shares of common stock outstanding rather than the 370 million shares that are actually in stockholder hands, each share would have 10 times the claim and be worth approximately 10 times as much as the current market value. That is, each share would be worth 10 times the current price if Coca-Cola's total assets and earnings remained at exactly the same level.

As owners of a business, common stockholders have a financial interest that is secondary to virtually every other individual or group with a relationship to the firm. Payments to suppliers, employees, lenders, the Internal Revenue Service, and the local tax authority all have priority when it comes to cash distributions of the firm's money. In most respects, common stockholders are residual players in a firm's operation, in that they have a claim to whatever is left after all of the other participants have been paid.

The residual status of common stockholders places them in an investment situation of significant risk at the same time that they are in a position to reap significant rewards from cash distributions and/or increases in the value of their investment. If a firm is able to prosper, make the necessary payments to all of the other players, and have a significant amount of funds left over, then the stockholders find themselves in a very attractive situation. On the other hand, if very little cash remains or if the firm is unable to fulfill its obligations to the other players, then the stockholders will be in a very undesirable situation. It is the risky environment of the stockholder's position that creates the possibility for large returns.

The cash that remains after all other obligations of a business have been met is likely to benefit the stockholders whether a firm's management decides to pay all, part, or none of the cash to the owners. The cash distributed as dividends can be used by the stockholders to spend or reinvest as they see fit. Because nearly all dividends are considered taxable income, stockholders are able to spend or reinvest only what remains after taxes. Cash retained by the business can be used to acquire additional assets or pay off debt early.

Managements that prefer to reinvest cash in new assets rather than pay dividends to stockholders tend to increase the value of their firm's common stock at a more rapid rate than managements that distribute large dividends. Additional assets should result in even greater revenues and profits in future years. This connection can be tricky. If the additional assets do not produce sufficient future earnings and cash flows, there is no reason to expect that the value of ownership will increase, and the stockholders would have been better off receiving cash dividends.

Because a stockholder's financial rewards are primarily a function of a firm's ability to generate cash for dividends or reinvestment, the projected earnings and cash flows of a business are very important to the value of its stock. In general, the stock of a firm with good prospects for earnings and cash-flow growth will sell at a relatively high multiple to its current earnings. This price-earnings ratio (the market price of the stock divided by current or projected earnings per share of common stock) is a financial variable frequently used by stock analysts to determine if a stock is undervalued or overvalued. On the other hand, if the prospect of future earnings growth is poor or, at best, mediocre, the current price-earnings ratio is likely to be modest in comparison with the common stocks of firms expecting more rapid growth.

PURCHASING-POWER RISK

Purchasing-power risk for common stockholders relates to the uncertainty of return that results from the possibility that cash distributions and the market value of stocks will be depleted by unexpected inflation. The more these distributions and market values react positively to changes in inflation (i.e., the more they increase when inflation increases) the less the purchasing-power risk of holding a particular stock. At the opposite extreme, if a stock's cash distributions and market value tend to be unaffected by unexpected inflation, then an investor will experience considerable uncertainty over the real rate of return that will be earned.

How Common Stocks React to Inflation

In general, common stocks offer significantly more protection against unexpected inflation than do investments that make fixed payments. This does not mean that dividend payments to stockholders and the market values of common stocks will immediately change to offset the effects of inflation. Such changes are unlikely to occur. Over a period of years, however, many businesses and, thus, the common stocks of these businesses have the capacity to partially or fully protect investors against losses in purchasing power from unexpected increases in the prices of goods and services. Exhibit 5–1 illustrates the recent history of the Standard & Poor's 500 Index on both a reported and an inflation-adjusted basis. It is important to note that dividend income from the 500 stocks is not included in the average.

Without considering the possibility of increased dividends or changes in the market value of the assets a firm owns, inflation has a negative effect on common stockholders. The loss results from the devaluation in real terms of dividends and the market value of the security. A given dividend or stock price has less purchasing power because of consumer price increases.

The protection that common stocks offer against unexpected inflation stems from owners' claims against assets and earnings, two variables that are likely to benefit from inflation. There is no reason to expect that all businesses suffer during periods of inflation. In fact, corporate assets may increase in value as managements are able to raise the prices of their products or services to produce larger profits. Increased profits, in turn, can be expected to lead to increased cash distributions for stockholders and/or the acquisition of additional assets. In other words, unexpected inflation can actually produce benefits to the stockholders of some firms.

Expected inflation is factored into the prices of common stocks. For example, at any particular time oil stocks are priced to reflect the market prices expected for petroleum and its refined products. Likewise, the market price of General Motors' common stock reflects investor expectations relative to future automobile prices and the costs of producing these vehicles. Thus, it is unexpected inflation (or lack of expected inflation) that has the potential for

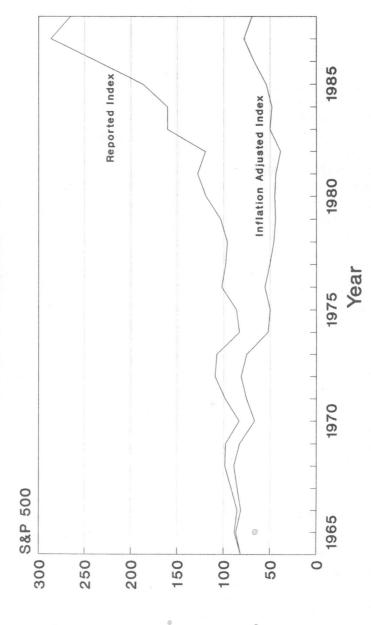

Exhibit 5–1
Stock Prices: Nominal and Real

producing changes in dividends and market values that affect the returns earned by common stockholders.

The Importance of a Firm's Line of Business

The effect of inflation on a firm's earnings and asset values depends in large part on the kind of business in which a firm is engaged. A business that produces goods or services for which it is relatively easy to raise prices may find that unexpected increases in inflation are fairly painless or perhaps, even desirable. The stockholders are thus likely to avoid much of the pain associated with inflation, although there is no reason to expect that dividends and the stock price will always move in proportion with inflation.

Another important aspect of the extent to which a business will be able to compensate for unexpected inflation is the mix of the resources it employs to produce goods and services. Businesses that use large amounts of labor or significant quantities of price-sensitive materials are likely to discover that, proportionately, their costs increase more than the general rate of inflation. Even though these firms can raise the prices of their goods and services, they may find that cost increases outrun revenue increases, so that earnings are penalized.

On the other hand, firms that use large amounts of fixed assets may find that their expenses increase only marginally, at least over the short or intermediate term. To a large extent these businesses are able to isolate costs from unexpected inflation, so that profits actually show gains during periods of inflation. Stockholders, in turn, may discover their own position improves in real terms, because the earnings and asset values on which they have a claim increase more rapidly than dollar values are depleted by inflation.

Common Stocks That Reduce Purchasing-Power Risk

The ideal common stock to offset the effects of unexpected price inflation is that of a company able to increase the price of its product or service at the same time that its costs remain relatively stable. Such a combination may sound too good to be true, but there are businesses considered to be relatively good inflation hedges because they possess these qualities. Most natural-resource companies are examples. Unexpected inflation can be expected to produce increases in petroleum prices, precious metals prices, lumber prices, and land prices. Companies owning these assets will find that their revenues increase, frequently by more than the rate of inflation. At the same time, many natural-resource companies have relatively moderate labor expenses, which means that their costs should increase at a fairly moderate rate. The result is that many natural-resource companies are likely to benefit from inflation.

Companies that have monopoly or near-monopoly positions in the goods or services that they provide generally find it easier to pass along increases in costs. For example, drug companies earn a considerable portion of their profits from products on which they have valuable patents. Without effective competition, firms find it relatively easy to raise prices, and they may not have much explaining to do for customers who are becoming accustomed to price increases in many things they buy.

On the other hand, firms that face heavy competition or that have their prices regulated may find it very difficult to operate in an inflationary environment. Public utilities, which have to justify rate increases to public authorities, are likely to find that their price increases lag behind inflation. As a rule, stockholders of these companies suffer significant purchasing-power risk.

INTEREST-RATE RISK

Although common stockholders receive dividends rather than interest payments, interest-rate risk is a very significant threat facing nearly all of these investors. The risk is that the rate of return earned by the common stockholder will be uncertain because of unexpected movements in interest rates. Mostly, this variation in the investor's rate of return involves a change in the market price of the common stock. To a lesser extent, it may also stem from a change in dividend distributions.

How Common Stocks React to Interest-Rate Changes

Except in unusual instances, increases in interest rates produce declines in common stock prices. The reason is that higher interest rates result in investors demanding higher rates of return from common stocks. The greater the unexpected rise in interest rates, the greater the pressure for a downward movement in stock prices. The recent history of the inverse relationship between stock prices and long-term interest rates is illustrated in Exhibit 5–2.

Chapter 2 showed that the rate of return demanded from common stocks is partially a function of the risk-free rate of return. The greater the return that investors can earn on risk-free assets, the higher the rate of return these investors will demand from common stock investments. Thus, if the risk-free return rises, investors will demand a higher return from common stocks, and common stock prices must fall to provide this higher return.

At any time, common stock prices already encompass current interest rates and investors' expectations as to future interest rates. For example, if investors expect interest rates to climb during the next year, common stock prices will already reflect an expected increase in rates. Because interest-rate expectations take into account inflationary expectations, stocks also already include current consumer price increases and expected future changes in consumer prices in the market prices at which the stocks trade.

Expectations regarding interest rates are already incorporated into stock prices, so it is unexpected changes in interest rates that move the prices of common stocks. In general, if interest rates unexpectedly move upward, then there will be pressure for common stock prices to fall. Conversely, if interest rates decline unexpectedly, then common stock prices can be expected to increase.

How Interest-Rate Changes Can Affect Dividend Payments

Interest-rate changes can affect a firm's dividend payments through changes in revenues and in costs. For example, if a firm's revenues depend heavily on interest income, then reductions in interest rates are likely to penalize earnings and produce the prospect of reductions in dividend payments to stockholders. While changing revenues because of interest-rate changes are a risk investors face, this uncertainty is more properly classified under business risk and will be discussed later in this chapter.

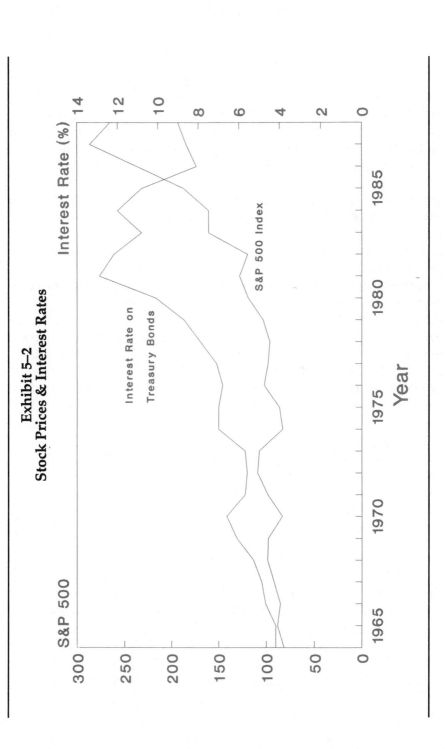

Exhibit 5-2
Stock Prices & Interest Rates

On the cost side, interest-rate changes can produce significant changes in interest expense if a firm is a heavy borrower. Thus, rising interest rates create greater interest expenses that penalize earnings, which brings with it the possibility of reductions in dividend payments. Conversely, reductions in interest rates will result in higher earnings that support increases in dividend payments to stockholders. Just as revenue changes are more appropriately discussed under business risk, however, changes in interest expense are considered part of financial risk and will be discussed later in this chapter.

The potential effect of interest-rate changes on common stock prices was demonstrated in the extended bull market that commenced in August 1982. The significant decline in interest rates that followed the very high real rates of the late 1970's and early 1980's brought with it an upward surge in stock prices that even the most optimistic investors could only dream about. While the bull market was also accompanied by one of the longest business expansions on record, the major decline in both short-term and long-term interest rates helped push virtually every broad-based stock average to historic highs.

Common Stocks That Reduce Interest-Rate Risk

Interest-rate risk is one of the most pervasive of all uncertainties for investors in common stocks. Because of the widespread effects of this risk, it is difficult to identify individual stocks that offer significant protection against the uncertain rates of return that result from unexpected changes in interest rates.

By and large, common stocks that return cash most rapidly should be least affected by changes in interest rates. Thus, stocks that provide investors with generous current income in the form of high dividend payments should be best suited to withstand unexpected increases in interest rates. Stocks purchased on the basis of expected increases in market price are susceptible to greater losses, because the major part of the investor's expected income does not result for a long time. The longer the time until cash is received, the greater the effect a change in interest rates will have on the investor's rate of return.

For example, the common stocks of cigarette and petroleum companies, which as a group tend to provide a relatively large portion of their expected return in dividend payments, will surely be depressed by increases in interest rates. However, these stocks may not be hurt as badly as common stocks that are expected to provide the major portion of their return in increased market values.

FINANCIAL RISK

An investor in common stock may be subject to substantial uncertainty of return because of financial risk. The severity of this risk depends on how heavily a business relies on debt and the firm's ability to service the interest expense and principal repayment required by the debt. Because common stockholders have a claim subordinate to the claims of the firm's lenders, the degree to which a business relies on debt becomes very important in determining the risk a stockholder faces.

Large amounts of interest expense greatly magnify changes in operating income into larger changes in the income earned by a firm's common stockholders. Because this income is used for the payment of dividends and is very influential in affecting investors' judgment as to the price at which a company's common stock should sell, its size and volatility are important in determining the stockholders' rate of return. If a firm has no interest expenses, then a 10-percent decrease in operating income (income after all operating expenses such as salaries, depreciation, and materials but before any financial expenses such as interest) will result in a 10-percent decrease in the net income available to common stockholders. For any firm using debt financing, the ratio of the percentage change in net income to the percentage change in operating income is greater than one. Thus, interest expense produces a more volatile net income and puts the stockholder in a more risky position.

Financial risk is relatively easy to minimize if an investor sticks to the common stocks of companies that employ small amounts of debt. There is no way to guarantee that a firm's management will continue to avoid indebtedness, of course, but a history of using debt only sparingly is a good indication that the firm is operated with a conservative financial philosophy.

The downside to choosing the stocks of firms that employ small amounts of debt is that earnings and dividend growth will likely lag behind other firms during periods of economic expansion. Fixed financial expenses permit a firm to earn a higher return on stockholders' money. Without this leverage net income tends to grow more slowly (and be less volatile) than would be the case if debt is a part of a firm's capital structure. Thus, the financial risk of owning common stocks can be selectively reduced, but it is reduced at the price of diminishing potential returns. Whether the reduction in risk is worth the loss of potential return is something only an individual investor can answer.

A number of popular financial publications including *Moody's Handbook of Common Stocks*, Standard and Poor's *Stock Reports*, and Value Line's *Investment Survey* include information on the extent to which publicly owned firms rely on debt. All of these publications are available in nearly any college library and in most public libraries.

BUSINESS RISK

Business risk is a significant uncertainty facing investors in common stocks, although the degree of risk varies considerably depending on the firm's business activities. Some industries produce revenues that are very volatile and, as a result, quite difficult to accurately predict. Because the earnings and cash flow of a company are so dependent on its revenues, volatile revenues result in uncertain earnings and cash flows. With common stockholders at the bottom of the line when it comes to the distribution or reinvestment of cash, a sudden decline in revenues can quickly turn a period of substantial profit and plentiful cash into a time of large losses.

Lenders have the cushion of knowing that their income from interest and the repayment of a loan are legal obligations. Common stockholders are in a much riskier position and may find that a business downturn will result in reduced dividends and a declining market value for their ownership. Thus, the potential for reduced returns because of uncertain revenues is of much greater concern for common stockholders than it is for bondholders of the same firm.

As a rule, business risk varies more by industry than by firms within an industry. For example, firms that manufacture capital goods (the machinery used to produce more goods and services) are in the same boat when it comes to the business risk their common stockholders face; that is, they face a pretty rocky sea. Revenues from the sale of capital goods are historically very volatile with periods when firms operate at full capacity followed by periods when it is difficult to sell additional capital equipment at distress prices. Common stockholders in these firms find that dividend increases are generally temporary and followed by a subsequent reduction.

Stocks of companies in unstable industries often go through substantial swings over a business cycle as the fortunes of the companies change. The business risk faced by these common stockholders may vary somewhat from firm to firm within an industry, but in a relative sense the differences tend to be significantly less than between industries. Investors owning the common stocks of firms that produce capital goods are subject to significant uncertainties of return because of business risk regardless of the individual firm in which they own stock.

Investors can minimize business risk by considering the business history of industries when selecting common stocks. Relatively stable industries such as food processing, life insurance, electric power, and grocery retailing generally subject stockholders to reduced return uncertainty because of business risk.

It is also important to exercise judgment in selecting individual stocks within an industry. An electric power company in the construction phase of a large nuclear plant subjects its owners to considerably more business risk than does an electric utility with only a small construction budget and minimal involvement with nuclear generation.

Investors concerned about business risk can reduce their exposure to this uncertainty by selecting the common stocks of firms that are diversified in several unrelated industries. A diversified company can generally count on one segment of the business taking up the slack of a downturn in another segment of the business.

Thus, the firm's common stockholders are sheltered from the ups and downs of a single industry. Owning the stock of a diversified company is essentially the same as building a diversified portfolio of common stocks in unrelated industries.

Another method of influencing business risk is to concentrate on the common stocks of companies that are industry leaders. By and large, companies that lead an industry in sales and profits are better able to withstand cycles in business activity than are smaller, undercapitalized firms that may have little customer loyalty. Selecting the industry leader in an industry with a history of volatile revenues still subjects a common stockholder to significant amounts of business risk, but it reduces this uncertainty below what it would be with a smaller firm in the same industry.

REINVESTMENT RISK

The uncertainty from owning common stocks caused by not knowing what return will be earned on cash payments is less than for fixed-income investments. The reduced uncertainty stems from the fact that most common stocks offer potential capital appreciation as an important part of their expected return. Because the return from capital appreciation does not involve any cash flows that must be reinvested, there is no reinvestment risk to a significant part of the return earned by common stockholders.

Reinvestment risk is relatively larger for investors who purchase the common stocks of firms that pay a large portion of earnings in dividends. These income stocks are generally purchased for their dividend yield, which means there will be cash payments that must be reinvested. Utilities frequently pay out a large portion of earnings in dividend payments and subject investors to significant reinvestment risk.

As previously noted, reinvestment risk is unimportant to someone who plans to use dividend payments for consumption purposes. An investor who needs current dividend payments to meet normal living expenses has no reason to be concerned about the return that could be earned on these funds. On the other hand, for individuals who acquire investments with the intent of reinvesting a considerable portion of the dividends they receive, reinvestment risk is an important consideration.

Another side to the reinvestment risk facing common stockholders is worth mentioning. That is, when a firm reinvests cash in additional assets in order to grow or become more efficient, the return that the firm is able to earn on these assets is a very important concern to common stockholders. If a company reinvests cash in assets that prove to be losers, earnings growth will be impeded and the firm's stock price is likely to suffer. Thus, while reinvestment risk is normally viewed in terms of the return an investor will be able to earn on reinvested cash, from the common stockholders' standpoint the risk should also consider the return the firm will earn on money reinvested rather than paid out in dividends. Viewed from this perspective, reinvestment risk for common stockholders is higher than when only cash distributions are considered.

MARKET RISK

Market risk is very important for most common stockholders. Common stocks tend to fluctuate over fairly wide price ranges resulting in unexpected losses in the event that shares must be sold on short notice. The greater the range over which a stock price fluctuates, the greater the uncertainty of the price that will be received in case it is necessary to liquidate.

For long-term investors in common stocks, market risk is relatively unimportant, although large swings in the market price of a stock can sometimes prove unsettling. If an investor anticipating a relatively long holding period of 10 or more years purchases common stocks, the weekly, monthly, or even yearly price fluctuations of a stock are of fairly minor importance. If uncertainty exists about how long a stock may be held and there is some possibility that shares may have to be sold on short notice, then the degree to which a stock's market price fluctuates becomes an important consideration.

Observing a stock's past price performance provides insight into the amount of market risk facing an investor. Individual stocks and the stocks of companies operating in particular industries tend to establish a history of price movements that permits investors to assess market risk. Thus, a careful examination of the price range of a particular stock over a period of years should provide a good indication of the relevant market risk.

Beta, a statistical measure of the degree to which a stock's returns are influenced by returns in the market, can also be used to assess a stock's market risk. As a rule, the greater the beta of a stock, the more market risk owning the stock involves. Appendix C gives an explanation of beta.

As a rule, the common stocks of companies that are market leaders are likely to subject investors to less market risk than are the stocks of second-tier companies. Likewise, newly issued stocks often go through wild price gyrations that produce great market risk. Thus, uncertainty from price fluctuations can be reduced by sticking to seasoned stocks of companies with relatively large capitalizations.

LIQUIDITY RISK

Liquidity risk varies significantly among the broad array of common stocks traded on the secondary market. Some common stocks have such great liquidity that the market can easily absorb very large transactions at a price virtually identical to the price of the previous transaction. Common stocks such as AT&T, General Motors, and Exxon trade hundreds of thousands of shares each day and offer great liquidity. An investor can easily sell several thousand shares without even a ripple in the stock price.

On the other hand, many issues of common stocks present investors with a real liquidity problem if a need arises to liquidate the securities in a hurry. The lack of liquidity can be fairly severe for stocks traded over the counter when there is only a single market maker. Essentially, a single firm acts as a dealer and calls the shots for the price at which a particular stock can be purchased and sold. Numerous unsuspecting investors run into this liquidity trap when they try to liquidate a very low-priced stock in a market that comprises no buyers other than the dealer.

As a group, stocks traded on the New York Stock Exchange tend to have greater liquidity than stocks traded in the over-the-counter-market. However, it is certainly not true that all of the stocks listed on the Big Board are more liquid than stocks traded over the counter. There are NYSE stocks with relatively limited activity, while there are OTC stocks that trade in volume every day. Still, listed stocks have market makers who are expected to act as buyers or sellers of last resort. Although OTC market makers post bids and ask prices, the big October 1987 decline illustrated that many of these quotes could have disappeared instantly when the dealers failed to answer their telephones.

A relatively easy way to ensure some degree of liquidity is to restrict investments to common stocks having a history of adequate trading volume. Most of the stocks listed on one of the organized exchanges or included in the National Association of Securities Dealers' National Market System have adequate trading volume to provide for the average investor's liquidity needs. Volume for individual stocks can be checked in many daily newspapers. Very light activity or occasional days of no trading are indications that there may be some difficulty in liquidating a large number of shares.

Investors who are concerned about liquidity are probably wise to avoid penny stocks and other securities that happen to be heavily promoted by some brokers. Stories of huge past gains and the potential for even bigger advances in the near future often turn out to be a cover for a security with a very limited secondary market. The quotations may come from rigged markets in which it is difficult to sell what has been purchased. Investors who desire liquidity in the common stocks they buy should think long and hard before purchasing stocks which are not traded on one of the larger organized exchanges and are not included in the National Market System.

SUMMARIZING RISK AND COMMON STOCKS

Compared to nonmarketable and fixed-income investments, common stocks are risky assets because they produce rates of return quite difficult to forecast. This blanket characterization is a generalization, however, for in certain respects common stocks may actually subject an investor to less risk than long-term bonds and long-term certificates of deposit. Also, the riskiness of individual common stocks spans a wide range. Some common stocks are very risky in nearly every respect. Other stocks are, by most measures, less risky to hold than many bonds and debentures issued in the spate of corporate takeovers that occurred during the 1980s.

One uncertainty in which common stocks can provide a degree of refuge is protecting investment returns from inflation. A company's productive assets are often able to produce additional profits during periods of general price increases so that common stockholders can benefit from increased cash distributions and market values. The transformation of general inflation into increased profitability depends on a variety of considerations such as the ability of a firm to pass price increases along to customers and the kinds of inputs used by the firm in producing goods and services.

While the unusually high inflation rates of the late 1970s initially harmed common stock prices, many companies were later to become the victims of takeovers and buyouts as investors judged that corporate assets were severely understated on the financial statements and were undervalued by investors. A significant portion of the change in the perceived value of these firms derived from the fact that prices of the goods and services produced and the replacement value of the assets owned had increased significantly during the earlier inflation.

In most respects other than providing protection from inflation, common stocks are relatively risky assets to own. Shares fluctuate in market value, dividend payments frequently change, and companies sometimes go out of business. Their products may be out of date, the economy may suffer a serious reversal, or interest rates on short-term loans may skyrocket. A variety of things can occur to cause grief and financial loss to someone who has the residual claim of a common stockholder. Interest-rate risk, financial risk, business risk, and market risk are all formidable uncertainties with which most common stockholders must cope.

The riskiness of a stockholder's portfolio of common stocks can be adjusted by careful selection of securities. Old-line firms with moderate amounts of debt and fairly large dividend payouts subject their owners to less uncertainty than do new stock issues and the stocks of firms in very unstable and highly competitive industries. Again, however, the severity of the risks that investors encounter in common stock investing varies, sometimes significantly, from one stock to the next. Even the stocks of companies operating in the same industry can have diverse risk characteristics.

The variety of the common stocks available for investors to purchase is so diverse that it is possible to locate a number of candidates that will fulfill any particular investor's needs with respect to risk. For example, if liquidity is important, there are hundreds of common stocks that provide more liquidity than all but the largest institutional investors will ever need. If an investor wishes to reduce financial risk, there are common stocks of companies that have incurred very little debt. If market risk is a concern, many firms have a history of relatively stable stock prices.

CONVERTIBLE BONDS

Although it may seem more appropriate to include convertible bonds in the previous chapter, it is not really possible to understand the risks of owning these hybrid securities until the uncertainties relevant to both bonds and common stocks have been discussed. Convertibles take on most of the risks of each category of security while tending to moderate these same risks. As a result, these securities appeal to investors who desire to straddle the fence between bonds and common stocks.

Characteristics of Convertible Bonds

Convertible bonds are debt securities an investor can exchange for something else, generally, a fixed number of shares of common stock of the same firm. Convertibles are issued as delayed equity financing with the expectation that the bonds will eventually be converted.

Companies have a variety of motives for issuing these bonds. For one thing, convertible bonds lower the interest rate at which the firm can borrow money compared to what would be paid if regular debt was issued. Also, the firm's managers may feel that the market price of the company's stock is currently depressed, and they do not want to sell new stock into a weak market. Thus, both investor and the issuer strike a compromise between debt and equity.

Convertible bonds pay semi-annual interest and provide for the return of principal on a stipulated date just as a regular bond. In fact, other than that the bonds can be exchanged for shares of common stock, convertible bonds are identical to the regular bonds issued by a corporation. Of course, the federal government, states, and local governments are unable to issue convertibles because no stock is traded in these organizations. Investors can lend money to the government but, despite what some cynics may think, you can't buy it. At least not in the normal financial sense of the word.

The number of shares for which a convertible bond can be exchanged is stipulated at the time the bond is issued and nearly always stays constant until maturity. If an investor decides to exchange a bond for shares of stock, all claims to the principal and to any further interest are given up. Also, the exchange is permanent and cannot be reversed by either the issuer or the investor. If the stock performs poorly and the bond is not exchanged for shares of stock, the bond will mature on the predetermined date and interest payments will cease. The exchange is at the option of the investor, who may convert at any time prior to maturity or to an early call.

In general, changes in the market price of the convertible bond will parallel changes in the price of the shares into which the bond is convertible. The higher the price of the stock and the higher the market value of the bond, the more the bond assumes the behavior of the common stock. However, if the stock performs poorly the convertible will be priced primarily on the discounted value of its interest and principal. For example, a $1,000 principal amount bond with a coupon rate of 9 percent and convertible into 50 shares of common stock currently priced at $4, will be valued more for the interest payments and eventual return of principal than for the conversion value of the common stock. This particular bond will exhibit characteristics virtually identical to a regular bond, as long as the stock price is in such a depressed state. If the stock rises to $30, the bond should sell for at least $1,500 because this is the value of the 50 shares of common stock for which the bond can be exchanged. At this point the value obtainable from conversion becomes more important than the interest and principal payments.

The Risks of Owning Convertible Bonds

The owners of convertible bonds are subject to purchasing-power risk but not to the same extent as are regular bondholders. Because common stocks provide some protection against losses in purchasing power caused by general price inflation, bonds that can be exchanged for shares of common stock furnish some of this same protection. If a business is able to take advantage of an inflationary environment so that the value of its own shares of ownership increases, convertible bonds of the same firm should also increase in price.

The degree to which the investor is protected against purchasing-power risk depends on the degree of protection the stock provides and the extent to which the price of the bond responds to price changes of the stock. If the bond is selling primarily on the basis of its common stock value, then the bond will provide virtually the same protection against purchasing-power risk as the common stock. On the other hand, if the convertible trades primarily on the basis of its value as a bond, the conversion feature will provide less protection against unexpected price inflation.

A convertible bond will experience considerable price volatility because of interest-rate changes if the bond trades primarily on its value as interest-bearing debt. If the convertible is valued primarily for its conversion value in stock (i.e., as in the above case when the stock sold for $30 per share), the bond will respond to interest-rate changes much as the stock will. If the stock into which the bond is convertible is strongly influenced by interest-rate changes (as in the case of the common stock of electric utilities), then there will be considerable exposure to interest-rate risk from holding the convertible.

Because bondholders have a legal claim to a stream of interest payments and the repayment of principal, convertibles generally subject investors to less business and financial risk than does the common stock of the same issuer. At the same time, convertible debt frequently has a subordinated claim to other lenders, which makes it relatively risky debt. Thus, convertible bonds have less business and financial risk than common stock of the same issuer, but they may have more business and financial risk than the common stock of a different company.

By and large, convertibles produce less market risk than common stocks but more market risk than regular debt of the same issuer. Because the market value of a convertible is influenced by market swings in both the bond market and the stock market, it is generally subject to smaller swings than either one individually.

The liquidity risk of a convertible varies considerably, depending on the particular issue being considered. Some convertibles trade actively and are very easy to resell. Other issues trade infrequently and may require a buyer or seller to give on the price if a quick sale is required. Liquidity risk is relatively easy to determine by checking on past market activity. One extra consideration is that as more bonds of an issue are exchanged for shares of the underlying common stock, there will be fewer bonds to trade in the secondary market. Thus, the liquidity of an issue may deteriorate over time.

In summary, convertible bonds are a compromise security that take on the risk characteristics of both long-term bonds and common stock. The risks applicable to a particular bond depend on whether the convertible is trading primarily on its conversion value into shares of common stock or on the basis of its claim to interest and principal. Convertibles that trade primarily on their conversion value are more heavily influenced by the risk characteristics of the stock than the risk characteristics of bonds. The opposite is true for convertibles that trade primarily on their value as bonds.

STOCK OPTIONS

From once being a little-known specialized security used almost exclusively by professional investors, stock options have come to be among the most popular of all investment vehicles. The thrust for this popularity stemmed from the organized trading of standardized option contracts on the Chicago Board Option Exchange (CBOE) in 1973. The standardization of stock options allowed an investor to close out an option position by making an offsetting trade in an identical contract. In other words, an investor who bought a particular option would be able to resell the security prior to its expiration date. Likewise, investors who sold options short would be able to purchase an identical option and terminate their obligations to either purchase or deliver shares of a particular stock. Prior to standardized options, the contracts had virtually no liquidity. Subsequent to 1973, trading in stock options has exploded, with listings being expanded to other exchanges. Options on futures contracts have since been added and have enjoyed immense popularity.

Characteristics of Stock Options

The two major types of stock options are calls and puts. A call gives the investor the right to purchase 100 shares of a particular stock at a fixed price until a specific date. An investor who purchases a call option locks in a price on 100 shares of stock for a predetermined time. A put option gives an investor the right to sell 100 shares of a particular stock at a fixed price until a specific date. A put locks in a price at which to sell stock rather than a price at which to buy stock. Both puts and calls provide the investor with the right, but not the obligation, to use the option. Stock options are created, or "written," by other investors who wish to earn income from selling the options. The writers then become obligated to sell (if a call has been sold) or purchase (if a put has been sold) the stock if and when the owner of the option decides to exercise the put or call.

Puts and calls derive their values from the values of the stock that they can be used to sell or purchase. Stock options pay no dividends or interest and expire without any value if not used by the expiration date. The value of a call option is directly related to the value of the underlying stock (i.e., the option value increases when the stock value increases) and the value of a put is inversely related to the value of the underlying stock (i.e., the option value increases when the stock value decreases). Option values are also affected by the time remaining until expiration, the price volatility of the underlying common stock, the dividend payments of the underlying common stock (individual dividend payments cause the market price of a stock to decline), and the market rate of interest.

Risks of Buying and Selling Options

Depending on how options are used, investors can be subject to substantial risks. Losing the entire amount spent to purchase a call option or a put option is not an unusual event. Investors who write options are subject to the possibility of losing substantially more than the premium received. Option prices are volatile to the point that their relative values change by a multiple of the change in the underlying stock. Thus, anything that can bring about a change in the price of the underlying stock in a short period of time has the potential for producing great losses (or profits) for the owner of a stock option. On the other hand, purchasing-power risk is of no great concern to an investor in options, because put and call options typically expire in a matter of a few months.

If an option position is established in combination with another investment that is purchased or is already owned, the result may be that an investor's uncertainty is reduced. For example, an owner of 500 shares of VSC common stock may purchase five puts on this stock and guarantee a selling price in the event that the market price of the stock declines. Thus, the puts act as price insurance on the investment position. Likewise, investors will frequently write calls on stocks that they own to generate additional income. Because the stock is already owned by the writer, the required shares can be delivered in case the option buyer exercises the call.

Many options are lightly traded, so that there may be a significant element of liquidity risk to closing out a position. The amount of risk depends on the size of an investment position relative to normal trading activity in the option. The price volatility and lack of liquidity produce a situation in which investors may wish to use limit orders to reduce the possibility that an execution will occur at a price considerably different from what an investor expects.

While options can be used in conjunction with other securities to reduce the overall risk of an investment position, it is unlikely that this is the use to which most individual investors put options. By and large, stock options tend to be very risky investments suitable for investors seeking unusually high returns while understanding that a possibility of substantial losses exists.

Brokers and investment advisors frequently make the case that options expose investors to less risk than an investment in the underlying common stock, because the potential losses are smaller. This is true only for the dollar amount of the loss. On a percentage basis, however, the potential losses on an option position are substantially higher than on an equivalent position in the underlying common stock. An investor stands to lose less on options only because less money is initially invested. From this standpoint, the investor also generally stands to make less than would be the case if the underlying stock was purchased. On a percentage basis, however, there is no contest; an investment in options is substantially riskier than an investment in the underlying stock.

The bottom line for investors is that stock options should be avoided by anyone who doesn't have a thorough understanding of the fundamentals and potential risks of these volatile investments. The short-term nature of options frequently results in heavy trading and high commissions that often work more to the advantage of a broker's bank account than an investor's brokerage account.

SELF-HELP QUESTIONS

1. What portion of your investment portfolio is composed of common stocks? How did you arrive at this proportion? Do you feel that it is appropriate?

2. Are your investment goals better served by growth stocks or income stocks? Are you considering tax consequences in your answer? To which of these categories do your current holdings of common stocks belong?

3. How can common stocks provide an investor with protection against unexpected inflation? How is it that some stocks are better inflation hedges than others? How would you rate your own stocks as inflation hedges?

4. What risks that are applicable to owning common stocks are of the greatest concern to you? What types of common stocks are most likely to minimize these risks? Do the stocks you now own reduce these risks?

5. If the stock market went into a severe decline, would you be most likely to acquire additional stocks or liquidate the stocks you now own? Which course of action do you feel would be most appropriate? When you purchase common stocks, do you set any price targets at which you will reassess whether to continue holding the stocks?

6. On what basis have you selected the stocks you now own? Did you consider the stocks you already owned when you made your most recent common stock acquisition? How did this stock fit in with the securities you already owned?

7. Do you feel that common stocks are more risky than fixed-income securities? In what ways? Can you think of any risks that are greater for the owner of a fixed-income security than for the owner of a common stock?

8. What are the advantages and disadvantages of owning convertible bonds as opposed to the common stocks into which these bonds are convertible? Do you think your needs could be better met by a convertible bond or equivalent shares of the common stock?

Chapter
Six

THE RISKS OF OWNING TANGIBLE ASSETS AND FUTURES

The luster of tangible assets was brightest during the inflationary years of the late 1970s. Gold, silver, real estate, investment-grade stamps and coins, and farm land made investors out of farmers and speculators out of investors. At the same time, financial assets such as common stocks, bonds, and certificates of deposit were considered investments with a past but no future. One major business magazine featured as its lead article a story explaining why the bond market was unlikely to recover from years of devastating losses. The rationale was that investors had suffered such a terrible and lengthy financial beating from holding fixed-income securities that they would no longer be willing to place their funds in long-term bonds. The relentless road of more inflation, rising interest rates, and falling bond prices had apparently brought a total collapse in one huge sector of the capital markets.

Despite what many individuals and institutions viewed as a permanent change in investors' attitudes toward tangible versus financial assets, it was not long before the investment climate was turned upside down, with financial assets regaining a position of respectability. The change brought with it a generally unfavorable environment for tangible assets. Diamonds may be forever, but their lofty prices are not.

Futures, while not actually tangible in nature, are frequently contracts for the delivery of tangible assets. Precious metals and agricultural commodities are two important categories of assets that have generated an active futures market. There are also futures contracts for foreign currencies, Treasury bills, and gasoline. Some of the risks applicable to investments in tangible assets also apply to futures contracts. In other ways, however, the risks to investors in these two types of assets are entirely different. Futures are covered in a separate section at the end of this chapter.

CHARACTERISTICS OF TANGIBLE ASSETS

Tangible investments include assets that can be seen and touched. Sometimes they can even be cuddled. Who hasn't looked at a brilliant gold coin and secretly desired to lovingly cradle it in the palm of the hand? Who hasn't wished to run their fingertips over the shimmering tail fin of a carefully restored 1957 Chevrolet? This desire of individuals to possess a particular asset is one of the important attributes that turns the asset into an investment. The more people who wish to possess the asset and the stronger their desire and greater their wealth, the more likely that the investment will appreciate in value.

Some tangible assets produce current income at the same time that they offer the potential for increases in value. For example, a farm may be desirable for the current income it produces at the same time that it is valued, in part, because of the possibility that portions of the land are in the path of economic development.

Other tangible assets produce no current income but are valued because investors feel that in future years the assets will be sought by other investors. Precious metals, stamps, and art are often highly valued assets, despite the fact that they produce no current cash flow for the owners. Of course, some individuals may receive a great deal of personal satisfaction from owning assets such as these. Other investors purchase these tangible assets only because they feel that the assets can be resold at a higher price at some point in the future. In some cases, assets may also provide their owners with certain tax advantages.

There are a variety of methods of investing in tangible assets. The most straightforward is to simply purchase an asset and take delivery. This is the procedure that generally takes place in the case of stamps, coins, and art, for example. An investor may prefer that an asset be held in safekeeping with only a certificate being issued to show proof of ownership. This may be desirable in the case of an asset too bulky or expensive to deliver. It may also be preferred in instances when an asset must be examined prior to delivery. If the asset is immobilized so that it does not physically change hands with each sale, it is only necessary to appraise the asset one time. Immobilizing an asset and delivering a certificate of ownership also eliminates the need for the investor to store the asset.

One of the major difficulties encountered when investing in tangible assets is judging quality. Unlike financial assets, which trade in standardized units, tangible assets are generally similar but not identical. Even small differences in quality are important, because they can result in wide differences in market value. For example, the most valuable Lincoln penny is the 1909 issue from the San Francisco mint with "VDB," the designer's initials, inscribed on the bottom of the reverse side. Despite the scarcity of this coin, quality in collector coins is so important that one of these coins in very good condition is worth many times more than one that is in only fair or poor condition. Thus, two coins with the same mint markings can bring vastly different prices upon resale. The importance of these quality differences are applicable to other tangible investments from stamps to baseball cards.

THE RISKS OF INVESTING IN TANGIBLE ASSETS

In general, it is quite difficult to accurately forecast the return that a tangible asset will earn. In large part this risk stems of the fact that most tangible assets produce no cash until they are sold. Thus, the estimated return depends entirely on a forecast of the asset's price in the future, often the distant future. With respect to certain individual risks, tangible assets provide a degree of protection in comparison to financial assets. In most respects, however, tangible assets subject individual investors to substantial risk.

The causes of uncertain returns from holding tangible assets are very different from the causes affecting returns on financial assets. Because the risk characteristics are so different, understanding the differences will assist an investor in putting together a portfolio that provides protection against most of the uncertainties that can devastate an individual's investment position.

Purchasing-Power Risk

Because most tangible assets produce no cash flow other than the funds received from selling the asset, only increases in the market value of the asset are available to offset potential losses from reduced purchasing power. Thus, the potential of substantial purchasing-power risk exists if the market value of the asset is not directly related to inflation.

By and large, tangible assets provide substantial protection from purchasing-power risk. In fact, more than anything else, it is the fear of inflation that drives investors from financial assets to tangible assets. When inflation fears subside, investors move back into financial assets.

Like financial assets, tangible investments are priced to include a consensus expectation of inflation. Gold selling at $420 per ounce and silver selling at $5.75 per ounce each incorporate some level of inflationary expectations. Changes in these expectations will cause the market price of gold to increase or decrease depending on the direction and extent to which these investor expectations change. If events cause investors to adjust inflationary expectations upward, money will flow into investments perceived to provide protection against higher consumer prices. The increased demand brought about by an upward revision of inflationary expectations will cause the prices of both gold and silver to rise. The effect on most other tangible assets will be similar, and prices for old coins, rare stamps, diamonds, art, and real estate will also tend to rise. These inflation-based increases in market values will then act to offset the higher inflation. It is the price adjustments that occur as a result of changes in inflationary expectations that allow tangible assets to reduce the risk investors face from unexpected inflation.

Tangible assets are not homogeneous, and there is no reason to expect that all of these investments will react in an identical manner to a change in inflationary expectations. Even the prices of different assets within a similar grouping do not always change proportionately. For example, there is no reason to expect gold, silver, and platinum to react identically when inflationary expectations change. The market prices of all three precious metals are likely to move in the same direction, but it would be improbable that they would move proportionately.

In summary, tangible assets generally provide investors with substantial protection against purchasing-power risk. The link between inflation and tangible asset values is so strong and the protection is so great that investors frequently use these investments not just to offset reductions in purchasing power, but to make a profit from inflation. These investors feel that inflation-induced increases in the price of the asset will actually exceed the rate of inflation that causes the asset to appreciate in value.

Interest-Rate Risk

Increases in the rate of interest penalize the market values of all assets, including those of a tangible nature. Because of this negative relationship between asset values and interest rates, the uncertainty of return caused by potential changes in interest rates is a serious risk facing investors in tangible assets.

First, higher interest rates cause the market to demand a higher return from tangible assets, which causes their prices to fall. This downward pressure on prices is especially severe with tangible assets, because they typically produce no cash flows to reinvest at the higher interest rate. It is one thing to sit on $50,000 worth of gold when money-market funds and certificates of deposit are returning 6 percent. It is something else entirely when alternative investments are returning 12 to 14 percent. An increase in the rate of interest from 6 percent to 12 percent will make an investor reconsider whether owning an asset that produces no current income is really a good idea.

If borrowed funds are used to support the purchase of the asset, it is not the opportunity cost that is important as much as it is the cost of financing. Most investment borrowing is at variable rates tied to the prime rate, so when interest rates rise, the cost of carrying the investment increases. With no cash flow to cover payments on the loan, a higher interest rate can prove to be very damaging.

Whether borrowing or cash is used to fund the purchase of a tangible asset, higher interest rates have the same effect of making a significant dent in the demand for these assets by making them more expensive to hold. A reduction in demand will produce a corresponding decline in the market price.

The limited number of tangible assets that produce periodic cash flows for their owners are also negatively affected by rising interest rates. This would include an investment in rental real estate, for example. Even though the market values of these assets will be affected, there should be less downward pressure on their market values, because they generate cash that can be reinvested at the higher return. This analysis is similar to comparing a zero-coupon bond with a bond that pays regular interest. The market value of the zero-coupon variety (i.e., the tangible asset that provides no periodic cash flows) is affected to a much greater extent by changes in interest rates than is the market value of the regular bond.

A previous section showed how inflationary expectations are an important consideration in determining the risk-free rate of interest. Because these inflationary expectations are a component of the risk-free rate, as expectations change, the risk-free rate of interest changes in the same direction. If inflationary expectations rise dramatically, the risk-free rate of interest will generally rise dramatically.

Higher inflationary expectations, when considered in isolation, frequently bode well for investors in tangible assets, since these expectations are likely to push the prices of the assets upward. Unfortunately, the higher interest rates that accompany a more pessimistic inflationary outlook have the effect of driving the market values of all tangible assets downward. Thus, the forces of inflation and interest rates work at cross purposes in influencing tangible asset values. The tug of war between the two forces will sometimes be won by inflationary expectations, and tangible asset prices will rise. At other times, interest-rate changes may overpower changes in inflationary expectations, and the market values of tangible assets will fall.

Because of the relationship between inflationary expectations and interest rates, rising interest rates do not present the same risk for owners of tangible assets as they do for investors in financial assets. The market values of tangible assets tend to be boosted sufficiently by rising inflationary expectations so that the downward pressure from rising interest rates is more than compensated for.

Financial Risk

Unless an investor borrows funds to finance an investment, there is no financial risk to owning tangible assets. Financial risk applies to uncertainty over an ability to meet financial commitments. Generally, this concern applies to the institutions that issue paper claims to investors. In the case of tangible assets, no similar obligation exists on the part of an issuer. Investors purchase tangible assets and generally have no further interest in the financial position of the seller.

If an investor borrows funds to finance ownership of a tangible asset, there is a risk that difficulties may arise in repaying the debt. Funds borrowed to pay for these types of assets can be a problem, because most tangible assets provide no periodic cash flows to assist with required loan payments. The financial risks for an investor who borrows to purchase a tangible asset depend on a number of factors including the portion of the purchase price financed, the type of loan made, and the volatility of the asset's market value. For example, if a tangible asset with a history of very large price swings is used as collateral for a loan, a real risk exists that the asset will decline so much in price that the lender will liquidate the asset to recover the principal on the loan.

Borrowing to purchase tangible assets should be done with great care. In fact, in most instances it shouldn't be done at all. With certain assets such as income-producing real estate, the risk is not as great as it is with tangible assets like precious metals, collectibles, and undeveloped real estate. Because most borrowing to finance these types of purchases entails a loan with a variable interest rate, the risk to the investor who borrows is that much greater. Rising interest rates produce a higher carrying cost on the loan at the same time that they tend to have a negative effect on the market value of the asset.

Business Risk

As with financial risk, business risk is typically thought of differently when examining tangible assets than when investigating financial assets. In both cases this risk refers to uncertain returns caused by the unpredictable revenue and cost streams of a firm or industry. Because tangible assets are normally purchased with the investor taking possession of the asset, there may be little concern on the part of the investor with the business fortunes of the individual seller.

On the other hand, there may be considerable concern about the unique factors that affect the particular industry from which the asset originates. The degree of concern depends on the particular type of tangible asset. Investors in platinum were rocked by the announcement of a potential substitute for platinum in catalytic converters used by the automotive industry. A number of years ago, investors in gold saw major declines in the value of their holdings when central governments announced upcoming sales of huge amounts of gold. Likewise, overbuilding of rental property can produce vacancies that penalize the owner of a rental duplex or an apartment building. These are examples of real business risk that have an effect on the rate of return an investor in a tangible asset will earn.

Certain tangible assets such as coins, stamps, and art tend to be subject to very minimal amounts of business risk. It is not as though the Treasury Department is going back to press and remint buffalo nickels with their original dates. Tangible assets prized more for their collectible value than for their value as an input in the production of a good or service subject their owners to very low levels of business risk compared to tangible assets such as precious metals.

Reinvestment Risk

Reinvestment risk depends on the time horizon applicable to a particular investment. As a rule, this risk is minor for investors in tangible assets, because these investments generally involve long-term holding periods during which the assets produce no cash flows that need to be reinvested. Reinvestment risk is more important for an investor involved with rental real estate but this is the exception rather than the rule. Investments such as collectibles, precious metals, and undeveloped real estate, essentially have no reinvestment risk if the investor plans a relatively long holding period.

Reinvestment risk becomes more important when an individual has a short time horizon. Suppose an investor draws funds from a money-market account paying 10 percent annual interest in order to purchase gold. If the individual expects to liquidate the asset within one year, the possibility exists that rates of return on money-market accounts will have dropped from 10 percent to 7 percent and that expected returns on other investments will have dropped proportionately. Thus, even an investor in tangible assets has reason for concern about rates of return that will be available on alternative investments when a tangible investment is liquidated.

Market Risk

The popularity of various types of tangible assets is constantly subject to major ebbs and flows, as investor sentiment rotates from one investment category to another. Because of the possibility of sudden changes in investor sentiment, large swings in the market values of tangible assets are a major risk investors face. Market risk is substantial for investments in nearly any type of tangible asset, but its severity varies because of the wide diversity in the individual characteristics of these assets.

Market risk is especially high when investing in collectibles such as art, coins, and stamps. It is even more severe with some of the more off-beat collectibles like baseball cards, antique automobiles, and political memorabilia. Even the more established tangible investments such as precious metals can exhibit wide market swings. An example is the surge in the price of silver to $52 per ounce in early 1980, only to be followed by prices equal to one-fifth of this amount during most of 1981. By the late 1980's the price of silver hovered in the $6 to $7 range. Fluctuations in the price of gold over the last several decades is illustrated in Exhibit 6–1.

Because tangible assets subject investors to such great market risk, individuals with short-term investment horizons are facing potentially large losses if they misread the market. Being required to liquidate an investment position in virtually any tangible asset during the bottom portion of a market cycle will almost certainly bring severe losses.

The danger that most investors encounter when they are considering the purchase of tangible assets is that these investments are frequently most enticing at exactly the wrong time. It is easy to be so carried away with an asset's market trend that investments are made at the top of market cycles and liquidations occur at the bottom of market cycles. Individuals view other investors earning high returns and rationalize that the cycle will continue long enough to make additional profits, even if they are getting in late. On the downside of a market cycle after a long bear market, a sense of hopelessness sets in, and investors become convinced that they should dump an asset before the price goes even lower.

The tendency for many investors to buy high and sell low is certainly not limited to tangible assets but, because tangible assets tend to have such pronounced market cycles, the losses from these investments are often quite large and the mistakes more costly.

Liquidity Risk

A potential lack of liquidity is an important consideration for investors in tangible assets. Many tangible assets have a very limited secondary market, so that investors face a large spread between the purchase price and the sale price. This spread requires that an investor experience a fairly substantial increase in the asset's market value so it can be sold at a price sufficient to recover the purchase price. For example, if a dealer marks up a diamond by 100 percent, then a stone must double in value before a buyer can sell at a price

Exhibit 6-1
Gold Price Range, 1968-1988

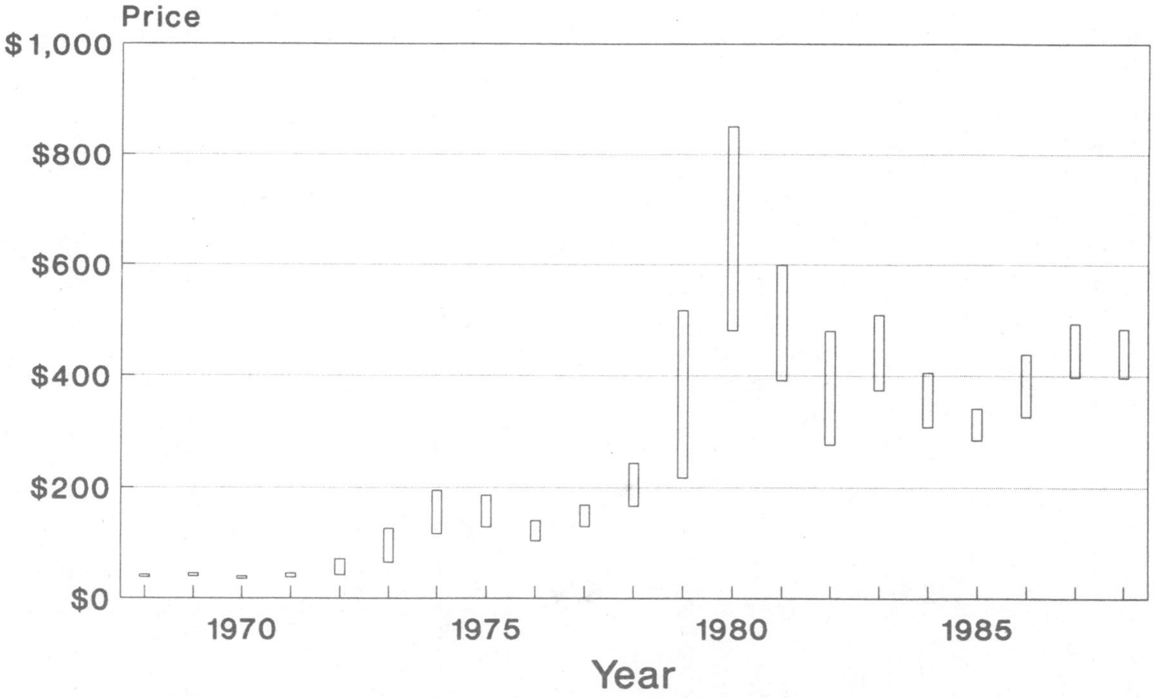

that will recover his outlay. Assuming that a dealer marks up an investment-grade stamp or coin by 25 percent, the asset must increase by this same percentage for a buyer to break even.

The size of an asset's spread relative to its price is an indicator of liquidity risk. The larger the spread relative to the price, the more liquidity risk an investor assumes. With most tangible assets the proportionate size of the spread is fairly large, indicating a high degree of liquidity risk. If you don't believe it, just talk to someone who was forced to sell an expensive engagment ring after it had been returned by someone who changed her mind.

With certain tangible assets having a fairly active secondary market, for example, one of the popular gold coins such as the Chinese Panda or the U.S. Eagle, liquidity is much greater and the relative spread is much more reasonable. Even here, however, an individual buying only one or two coins may discover a fairly large mark-up compared to someone who makes a more sizable investment.

SUMMARIZING THE RISKS OF OWNING TANGIBLE ASSETS

While tangible assets can offer significant protection against purchasing-power risk, in virtually every other respect most of these investments are very risky. Tangible assets tend to suffer from large fluctuations in market value, and they generally subject owners to significant liquidity risk. They often entail additional charges, such as premiums for insurance coverage or payments for safekeeping. An auxiliary problem is the possibility that the firm providing the safekeeping may fail. The bottom line to investing in tangible assets is to do it with great care and with a relatively long investment horizon. Buying tangible assets for quick resale is for experts and speculators.

THE RISKS OF INVESTING IN FUTURES

Futures contracts were at one time limited to agricultural commodities. Contracts on commodities such as oats, corn, pork bellies, coffee, and orange juice concentrate continue to enjoy great popularity, but futures are also now traded on currencies, precious metals, and stock indexes. (How times have changed. Moving one additional step from the underlying asset, investors can now buy and sell options on futures contracts.)

Characteristics of Futures Contracts

A futures contract is an agreement to make and take delivery of a specified quantity of an item on a certain date. The buyer of the contract agrees to take delivery and the seller of the contract agrees to make delivery. Because a contract calls for delivery, the price at which the contract trades determines the price of the item to be delivered. Thus, a futures contract permits both the seller and the buyer fix a price prior to the delivery time.

The primary, but not the only, determinant of the value of a contract is the market value of the item to be delivered. Thus, if the market price of the item to be delivered increases, the market value of the futures contract will also increase. Because both the buyer and the seller of a contract have already settled on a price, an increase in the value of the item underlying the contract benefits the buyer, who is to receive delivery. At the same time a price increase benefits the buyer, it harms the seller, who has agreed to deliver an item now worth more than when the contract was undertaken. Conversely, a decline in the price of the item scheduled for delivery benefits the seller of a contract at the expense of the buyer, who could have purchased the asset more cheaply by postponing a commitment.

Buying a futures contract does not mean that delivery of the underlying item has to be accepted, any more than selling a contract will eventually require a delivery. In fact, only a small proportion of these contracts are ever held until the settlement date when delivery is required. Rather, investors on both sides of a contract are likely to undertake an offsetting trade (i.e., take the opposite side of an identical contract) prior to the settlement date, thereby eliminating their respective obligations. The investor who has purchased a contract sells it, and the investor who has sold a contract purchases an identical contract. An active secondary market in futures contracts permits these offsetting trades.

Because investors on either side of a futures contract are required to put up only a relatively small portion of the value of the contract, a change in the contract's value magnifies the proportionate gains and losses of the participants. For example, if an investor puts up only 10 percent of the value of a contract, any movement in the market value of the contract (which is normally caused by a change in the price of the item) will magnify the effect on the participant's investment. A 10-percent decline in the market value of a contract will often wipe out the entire investment of the buyer at the same time it doubles the investment of the seller.

The Risks of Dealing in Futures Contracts

The risk from investing in futures contracts to a large extent depends on how the contracts are used. If a contract is used to offset another investment position, then a hedge is initiated and the risk of an investor's position is reduced. For example, a farmer concerned about the price that would be received for a crop at the time it was ready for delivery could sell a futures contract and guarantee a price ahead of time. Using a futures contract in this manner actually reduces risk. The farmer has locked in a price and essentially eliminated any uncertainty as to the revenues that will be received from selling the crop. Likewise, a business that plans to make a large purchase of goods from a foreign manufacturer in the home currency of the manufacturer runs the risk that the foreign currency may appreciate against the dollar before payment is due. To reduce the risk of buying the goods, the business can purchase a futures contract on the foreign currency, which would offset any changes in the rate of exchange between the dollar and the foreign currency.

An investor holding a large portfolio of common stocks can engage in a hedge by selling one or more futures contracts on a stock index. The short position in the futures contract protects against a downward movement in the market without requiring that the investor liquidate an entire portfolio of securities. The number of contracts and the stock index to use depend on the portfolio's size and composition, respectively.

Although using futures contracts for hedging reduces an investor's overall risk, the fact is that the majority of individual investors are interested in futures contracts not as hedging devices but as speculative investments. Individuals generally buy or sell contracts not to protect against movement in the market price of the asset but to profit from the movement. Nothing is wrong with this course of action, of course, so long as an individual understands the considerable risk it entails.

When futures contracts are invested in directly and not used as a hedge, they tend to be very risky. Price movements are sudden and unpredictable, so that it is not unusual for an investor to lose a substantial portion of the money invested in a futures position. While this loss may seem less serious because investors frequently put up only 10 percent of the value of a contract, the investor still stands to lose 100 percent of the amount that has been invested. In addition, if the market moves against an investor and the broker asks for additional funds, an investor may find himself throwing good money after bad.

Because of the great uncertainty of return that results from investing in futures for any reason other than hedging, individual investors would generally be wise to leave this investment sector to the professionals. Unscrupulous brokers have been known to entice unsuspecting investors with promises of great profits from investing in futures contracts. Such a volatile market does indeed offer the possibility of very large gains, but the down side is that there is also the chance of large losses. Futures trading is a game that the majority of investors would be wise to avoid altogether.

SELF-HELP QUESTIONS

1. What tangible assets with at least a modest amount of market value do you currently own? What is the total value of all the tangible assets you included, and what portion of your total assets (tangible and financial) do these assets make up? Do you think that this is the proper proportion?

2. What types of risks are tangible assets best at protecting against? What are the greatest risks of owning tangible assets? Which of the risks you have identified are most important to you?

3. As you move through your income-earning years toward retirement, what part do you see tangible assets playing in your investment portfolio? Is there any need for someone who is retired to own tangible assets?

4. What tangible assets tend to have the lowest transaction cost for the individual investor? To what extent should the cost of buying or selling be considered in deciding on tangible assets to acquire? What tangible assets tend to have high transaction costs?

5. What are the risks for an investor who has no tangible assets as part of an investment portfolio? For the investor who has concentrated on tangible assets at the expense of financial assets? How does the right proportion of tangible assets change over time?

6. How easy is it to determine the market values of the tangible assets that you own? When is the last time that you had reasonably precise values for these assets? Do you feel that the real returns on these assets have been satisfactory, considering the risk of owning them?

Chapter
Seven

THE RISKS OF OWNING NONMARKETABLE INVESTMENTS

In times of economic uncertainty, individuals tend to seek familiar surroundings for their money. No alternatives offer more familiarity than nonmarketable investments. These assets, which include such established investment alternatives as certificates of deposit, U.S. savings bonds, savings-type life insurance, and plain old passbook savings accounts, have been around long enough to offer a large degree of comfort to even the most skeptical investors. The stock market may fall out of bed, and rising interest rates may push bond prices through the floor, but the familiar and uncomplicated nonmarketable investments of old are still out there churning out their modest returns with unerring frequency.

When investors begin feeling their oats following an extended bull market in stocks or real estate or other more exotic investments, nonmarketable investments are generally out of favor to the point that individuals may be ashamed to admit to their friends that they have money invested in them. When the cycle turns, however, bruised investors return what remains of their funds to the conservative investment vehicles of the past.

Despite the unfailing periodic swings in the way investors view nonmarketable investments, these assets continue in their established role as the bread and butter products of the world's major financial institutions. And, although these investment alternatives are often considered to be primarily suitable for very conservative investors such as widows and orphans, nonmarketable investments offer stable returns with minimal risks and are viable investments deserving a place in many portfolios.

CHARACTERISTICS OF NONMARKETABLE INVESTMENTS

Investments are termed "nonmarketable" because they cannot be sold by one investor to another. Unlike investments in common stocks, corporate bonds, stock options, and futures contracts, a non-marketable investment is not customarily resold in order to obtain cash. An inability to resell nonmarketable investments does not mean that these assets lack liquidity since, in many cases, they offer the ultimate in liquidity. What it does mean is that a nonmarketable asset cannot be transferred at a profit to another investor. An investor may be able to take advantage of an increase in the market value of General Motors stock to sell shares at an appreciated price to another investor. The same potential for profits from non-marketable investments is not a possibility, because these assets cannot be resold at any price. On the positive side, nonmarketable assets cannot be sold at a loss.

Although nonmarketable investments cannot be resold, they can nearly always be liquidated for cash with the institution that issued the asset. For example, investors holding U.S. savings bonds can redeem the bonds for cash prior to the scheduled maturity. Investors who purchase certificates of deposit from savings and loan associations, credit unions, or commercial banks can redeem the certificates prior to maturity, although early redemption is likely to involve a penalty. The important point is that just because an asset cannot be resold does not mean that an investor holding the asset will be unable to liquidate the asset prior to a particular date.

Some nonmarketable investments actually have no maturity in the traditional sense. For example, money-market accounts at financial institutions permit investors to write a limited number of checks (normally three third-party checks per month) against the account balances. The ability to write checks means that, even though the institutions support the money-market accounts with loans and investments of varying maturities, the balances in individual accounts are available to investors on demand. The ability to write checks is the ultimate in investment liquidity, because an investor has immediate access to invested funds. In this case, there is no loss of value.

THE RISKS OF INVESTING IN NONMARKETABLE ASSETS

By and large, nonmarketable investments offer a combination of fairly modest returns along with substantial protection against loss of principal. As a result, these investments appeal mainly to investors who have an overriding desire to avoid potential losses, on the condition that they accept nominal rates of return. Nonmarketable assets are also appealing to investors who wish to balance other risky investment positions with assets that are liquid and that provide substantial protection against loss of principal from virtually any source.

Purchasing-Power Risk

Uncertainty caused by purchasing-power risk is not a great problem for the owners of most nonmarketable investments. These investments are not specifically designed to provide protection against unexpected inflation, but they are generally of such short duration that investors have access to their funds before great damage can occur to the purchasing power of the principal. The short maturities make it less likely that inflation will have time to exhibit the large unexpected changes necessary to produce uncertainty concerning the real rate of return that will be earned.

The major drawback with most nonmarketable investments as inflation hedges is that they generally provide nominal returns so close to the expected inflation rate that there is little room for error in the estimate for increases in consumer prices. During some periods these investments may provide nominal returns that are less than inflation. When inflationary expectations for the year ahead are in the 5- to 6-percent range, it is not at all unusual for nonmarketable investments to be yielding 7 to 8 percent. Assuming an investor pays taxes at a marginal rate of either 28 or 33 percent, the after-tax return may be less than the rate of inflation, which produces a negative real after-tax return. It doesn't take long to figure out that it's pretty difficult to get rich while earning a negative real after-tax return.

The longer the maturity of a fixed-income nonmarketable investment, the greater the possibility that unexpected inflation will affect the real rate of return. Thus, the longer the maturity the greater the purchasing-power risk. A certificate of deposit with a relatively long maturity of 8 to 10 years subjects an investor to considerable purchasing-power risk, because unanticipated inflation can substantially devalue the certificate's principal and interest payments. The principal of the CD will be at greatest risk from unexpected inflation, because it is returned in a single sum at maturity. Individual interest payments will suffer from varying degrees of purchasing- power risk, depending on the length of time before each is to be received. If the investor has chosen to have all interest payments automatically reinvested rather than paid, the degree of purchasing-power risk is substantially increased.

Owners of nonmarketable investments that pay a variable rate of return are compensated for unexpected changes in inflation, so that unexpected losses from reductions in purchasing power are offset by increased payments of current income. This protection from purchasing-power risk derives from changes in current interest rates in response to changes in inflationary expectations. The return paid on a variable-rate nonmarketable investment is altered to reflect changes in current rates of interest. Because the current interest rate incorporates an expectation for inflation, the nominal return on the investment is adjusted to reflect changed expectations.

U.S. savings bonds are an example of a nonmarketable investment that pays a variable current return keyed to the rate of interest on five-year Treasury bonds. Because increased inflationary expectations drive the yield on Treasuries upward, the interest payments made to holders of savings bonds will increase, even though the bonds were purchased on a previous date.

Protection against purchasing-power risk is also afforded to the owners of investment annuities, as long as the nominal return paid on the annuity is a function of some current short- or intermediate-term market rate of interest. On the other hand, an annuity that pays a fixed rate, has a maximum rate, or pays a return that is a function of some variable not influenced by changing inflationary expectations, provides no protection against purchasing-power risk.

The protection from purchasing-power risk provided by short-term nonmarketable investments is essentially identical to that offered by the variable-income alternatives just discussed. If market rates of interest change to reflect altered inflationary expectations, then any investment that permits an investor to earn the new rate will afford protection against purchasing-power risk.

Funds in money-market accounts and money-market funds can be expected to earn a return generally above, but very near, the rate of inflation. If inflationary expectations rise, then the return paid to account holders will likely rise. The returns on money-market funds sold by investment houses will rise, because interest rates on the investments owned by the funds will rise. The returns on money-market accounts at financial institutions will rise, because the institutions must compete with investment alternatives offering higher returns.

In summary, the uncertainty of an investor's real rate of return because of unexpected changes in inflation is not a great concern for owners of nonmarketable investments. The majority of these investments pay a return that tends to adjust for changes in inflation, so that investors are compensated with varying levels of income. On the down side, investors in nonmarketable investments are seldom able to earn returns that significantly outpace the rate of inflation, so the real return from these investments is generally quite low.

Interest-Rate Risk

Uncertainty from unexpected changes in market rates of interest is generally a minor concern for investors holding nonmarketable assets. The main reason for the unimportance of this uncertainty is essentially identical to that for purchasing-power risk. That is, the majority of nonmarketable investments have very short maturities. The result is that interest-rate movements have little or no effect on the market value of the principal, because the return paid to an investor adjusts to the new level of interest rates.

The income adjustment for changing interest rates varies somewhat among the array of nonmarketable investments. Returns on money-market accounts at financial institutions are generally altered on a weekly basis and roughly track the returns paid on Treasury bills, although the degree to which returns on these accounts are responsive to changes in interest rates varies substantially among the different institutions. If the rate paid on money-market accounts at a particular institution lags behind increases in market rates, immediate liquidity permits an alert investor to transfer an account's principal to an alternative investment.

Money-market funds pay a return that accurately tracks short-term interest rates, since it is the return paid on securities such as Treasuries and CDs that is passed through to the holders of these funds. Unlike money-market accounts, which generally adjust their returns weekly and may end up lagging changes in market rates, money-market funds adjust daily. There is no real interest rate risk for owners of money-market funds.

Nonmarketable investments that impose a penalty for liquidation prior to a specified date reduce the liquidity and subject the investor to at least some interest-rate risk. For example, certificates of deposit can be redeemed prior to maturity but typically require a penalty of 31 to 90 days' interest, depending on the original length of maturity. Because of the penalty, an investor owning a certificate is less likely to redeem the certificate early in order to take advantage of rising interest rates. Although the certificate does not decline in market value like a bond (there is no secondary trading of most certificates), the investor still cannot liquidate the investment position to take advantage of the higher interest rates without being penalized. As a result, the penalty makes the investor subject to a limited amount of interest-rate risk compared to a very liquid investment such as a money-market fund.

Previous mention was made of the fact that many of the large brokerage firms sell certificates of deposit for financial institutions. In selling these certificates the firms are acting as brokers in locating investors for the financial institutions. Fees are paid by the selling institutions rather than the investors. In addition to selling the certificates, the brokerage firms also make secondary markets in the certificates that have already been sold. Thus, an investor purchasing a certificate of deposit from a broker has an opportunity to resell the certificate prior to maturity at whatever price the market dictates. If market rates of interest are higher than the rate paid on the certificate, the value of the certificate in the secondary market will be less than the face value. The opposite change in value will occur if interest rates fall after the certificate is first sold. Certificates purchased in this manner have the characteristics of fixed-income securities rather than regular CDs. In fact, while brokers may indicate that it is preferable to purchase certificates in this manner, in some cases investors may be better off buying regular certificates that can be redeemed prior to maturity at a nominal penalty. On a certificate with a long maturity, there is a good chance that the penalty for an early redemption will be lower than the discount that would have to be accepted from a sale to another investor.

Investors who decide to have interest automatically reinvested at the base rate paid on a certificate of deposit subject themselves to additional interest-rate risk compared to investors who choose to have interest paid by check. Because there are no cash flows to reinvest until maturity, interest reinvestment locks the investor in at the original rate on interest payments as well as on the original principal. Automatic reinvestment benefits the investor if interest rates fall after the certificate is purchased, but the reinvestment produces a lower return if market rates rise after the purchase. A certificate that automatically reinvests interest is essentially the same as a short-term zero-coupon bond, because no interest payments are made for the investor to reinvest.

It may be in the best interest of the owner of a long-term certificate of deposit to accept the penalty of an early withdrawal in order to move funds into a new certificate with a higher interest rate. The profitability of such an action depends on the size of the penalty, the maturity length of the certificate, and the difference between the rate paid on the owned certificate and the rate paid on currently available certificates.

Investors purchasing annuity contracts can also be subject to interest-rate risk, depending on the specifics of the individual contract. Annuity contracts pay a current rate of interest on accumulated deposits that fluctuates with market rates over time. While this current rate is not guaranteed, the issuers generally specify a minimum guaranteed interest rate that is considerably lower than the current rate. In addition, many of the new contracts have a "bailout" provision that permits an investor to withdraw the principal and accumulated interest in the event that the insurance company fails to pay a specified minimum return.

Because annuity contracts pay a rate of return that is influenced by market rates of interest, investors are generally provided with at least some protection against uncertain real returns caused by unexpected interest-rate changes. On the other hand, the return an issuer is able and willing to pay on a contract may lag changes in market rates, so that an individual may wish to liquidate a contract and go elsewhere. If the rate is above the minimum specified in the bailout provision, the investor may have a problem. In fact, these contracts frequently entail large front-end load charges that make it uneconomical for investors to cash their contract in all but the most unusual of circumstances. As a result, most financial advisors suggest that deferred annuities be purchased only by individuals who expect to keep the contracts in force over a long period of time. The bottom line on deferred annuities with respect to interest-rate risk is that they provide some protection but not the unlimited protection that owners of money-market accounts enjoy.

Financial Risk

Financial risk is generally unimportant for investors in nonmarketable investments. Virtually all nonmarketable investments are either issued or backed by organizations that are financially secure. The strongest of these is the U.S. government, which guarantees the principal and interest on U.S. savings bonds. The government-sponsored agencies that insure deposits at insured banks, savings and loan associations, and credit unions protect individuals holding these investments from financial risk. Of course, the insurance may limit the amount of funds in a particular account or institution that are free from financial risk, but this problem can be overcome by opening accounts at different institutions.

Annuity contracts with insurance companies, while not insured by either the government or an agency of the government, nonetheless subject their holders to a relatively small degree of financial risk. Insurance companies are regulated by the states and restricted in the types of assets that they can acquire with policyholders' money. Investors can investigate an insurance company's financial strength prior to purchasing a contract in order to minimize the risk that the firm might encounter financial difficulties in the future.

Business Risk

Business risk is no more a concern for investors holding nonmarketable investments than is financial risk. The fact is that most nonmarketable investments subject their owners to virtually no business risk, and even those that do entail some risk, do so in minimal amounts.

Again, nonmarketable investments that are obligations of the U.S. government or that are insured by a government agency have no risk from uncertain revenues or costs of the issuing institution. At no time was this government backing put to a bigger test than during the savings and loan crisis of the late 1980s. The numerous failures of thrift institutions that resulted from a variety of causes, including faulty judgment, fraud, and an unfavorable economic environment, produced an estimated bailout cost of up to $100 billion. This cost was picked up by the taxpayers and the surviving institutions with the result that depositors at insured institutions saw the principal of their investments remain intact.

The investment uncertainty from business risk is greater at a private uninsured institution such as an insurance company, but even here the concern is relatively low. State regulations that produce an environment of minimal financial risk for investors holding deferred annuities also produce minimal business risk.

Reinvestment Risk

Reinvestment risk is perhaps the single most important uncertainty for individuals who place funds in nonmarketable investments. The cause of severe reinvestment risk among the owners of non-marketable investments is the same as that which produces minimal purchasing-power risk and interest-rate risk, and, as will be pointed out shortly, liquidity risk. That is, the majority of non-marketable investments have very short maturities, or they pay a return that is subject to being altered. Such an environment produces an investment that subjects its owners to significant uncertainty over the return that can be earned on cash flows.

Reinvestment risk is most severe for investments such as money-market accounts and money-market funds, which continually alter the returns that investors earn. These accounts may pay double-digit returns at the beginning of a year and yet pay no more than half that before the year has ended.

U.S. savings bonds and most investment annuity contracts have longer maturities but offer returns that change at predetermined intervals. Thus, even though the principal amount of the investment is not scheduled to be returned for many years, the investor is subject to reinvestment risk because the return paid on the principal is a function of the current market rate. Reinvestment risk on savings bonds and annuity contracts is reduced somewhat by a guaranteed minimum return. Still, because the returns paid on these investments are keyed to some market rate of interest that is constantly changing, an investor experiences significant uncertainty over the return that will be earned on one of these assets.

One nonmarketable investment with relatively small reinvestment risk is a long-term certificate of deposit, the same investment that produces the most interest-rate risk among these assets. Even here there is a difference, however. If an investor chooses a certificate that makes quarterly or semi-annual interest payments, then there will be uncertainty over the rate of return that these cash payments will earn. On the other hand, if an investor chooses a certificate in which the issuer automatically reinvests interest at the rate guaranteed on the original principal, then the degree of reinvestment risk depends solely on the maturity length of the CD. The longer the maturity for a certificate with automatic reinvestment, the lower the reinvestment risk.

Liquidity Risk

Investors holding most nonmarketable investments are subject to very little liquidity risk. The ultimate in liquidity is a deposit-type account that permits the investor to write checks on the balance. There is no liquidity risk to money-market accounts, NOW accounts, or passbook savings accounts, because an individual can withdraw the principal of the account without penalty and without loss of principal at any time.

A high degree of liquidity is one of the great advantages of most nonmarketable investments. Even a certificate of deposit with a relatively long maturity has little liquidity risk if the investor can redeem the certificate prior to maturity with only a small penalty. The larger the penalty, the more expensive it is to recoup the principal prior to maturity and the greater the liquidity risk. Still, even if a penalty of three to six months' interest is imposed, the cost of surrendering a certificate with a long maturity is nominal, and the liquidity risk is small.

The greatest liquidity risk among nonmarketable investments is with deferred annuities. These investments are relatively long term and may impose significant penalties on individuals who wish to access their principal or accumulated interest prior to a certain year. As previously mentioned, deferred annuities are primarily of interest to individuals who are planning to use the tax deferred accumulated funds to achieve some long-term goal such as retirement.

Market Risk

Market risk is not a concern for individuals who own nonmarketable investments. Assets such as certificates of deposit and U.S. savings bonds certainly go through cycles of popularity, but these swings in investment luster do not affect the investment values. The reason is simple: these assets can be redeemed at face value or very close to face value, and they do not trade in the secondary market. The result is an asset with a market value that remains unaffected by changes in the market.

SUMMARIZING RISK AND NONMARKETABLE INVESTMENTS

From the standpoint of the risks an investor must face, non-marketable investments seem nearly too good to be true. Essentially, these investments subject investors to virtually no risks other than an uncertainty as to the return that will be earned upon reinvestment. This isn't meant to minimize the importance of reinvestment risk, because for many investors this is a very important concern. Individuals who must live on their investment income may not worry about the rate of return that can be earned on periodic income payments, because they expect to spend virtually all of this income. These same investors, however, cannot rationally face a substantial uncertainty over the rate of return their investment principal will earn. Reinvestment risk that results because of a need to continually reinvest principal produces great uncertainty concerning the income payments that will be earned. Perhaps the best example of a nonmarketable investment that has a great amount of this risk is money-market funds that reinvest principal daily.

There may also be some liquidity risk with certain nonmarketable investments. Certificates of deposit have a nominal amount of this risk and deferred annuities have even more uncertainty in case a portion of principal is needed in a hurry. Overall, however, non-marketable investments offer a very high degree of liquidity to investors.

Interest-rate risk and purchasing-power risk are not a concern for investors holding most nonmarketable investments. The same is true for business risk and financial risk. In fact, taken as a group, there is probably less business and financial risk involved in owning these investments than there is in holding any of the other types of investment assets.

So what is the down side to nonmarketable investments? The main drawback of these investments is the modest return that is earned. There is virtually no chance of earning a return more than a few percentage points above the expected rate of inflation. Thus, the great certainty of return that is the great benefit of nonmarketable investments can also be a drawback if the certain return in real terms (adjusted for inflation) is owning close to zero.

SELF-HELP QUESTIONS

1. What type of investor is most likely to favor investments in nonmarketable assets? What part do these assets play in your own investment portfolio?

2. What is the difference in the returns that can currently be earned on insured certificates of deposit and Treasury bills or high-grade bonds of similar maturity? Do you feel that the difference in returns, if there is any, makes it worthwhile to invest in something other than certificates of deposit?

3. How can different institutions get away with paying different rates of return on certificates of identical maturity and risk? How many institutions did you check prior to investing in your last certificate of deposit?

4. In what ways is a U.S. savings bond a superior investment to a long-term certificate of deposit? In what respects is the U.S. savings bond more risky than a certificate of deposit?

5. Compared to marketable financial assets such as bonds and common stocks, what risks do nonmarketable investments minimize? Despite the lower returns that are normally paid to owners of nonmarketable investments, do you feel that these assets have a place in your own portfolio?

Chapter
Eight

CONTROLLING
INVESTMENT RISK

Whether it's unexpected inflation, unknown rates of return on the reinvestment of cash distributions, or the inability to liquidate an asset without incurring a significant price penalty, there are risks that lurk behind virtually all investment alternatives. Because of the widespread nature of these risks, there are few "sure things" in the world of investing.

The previous seven chapters identified the types of risks investors face and discussed the extent to which these risks are inherent in the ownership of specific investments. More than just identifying the risks of investing in various assets is required to produce an intelligent investment program, however. An individual must actually use this knowledge to construct a portfolio of assets that best suits his or her investment needs. There is no way to eliminate every possible risk, however, so even a carefully developed portfolio will subject its owner to at least some uncertainties.

Even though it may not be possible to avoid all potential risks, an investor must attempt to construct a portfolio that minimizes the uncertainties that can prove to be the most damaging to his or her individual requirements. Only by selecting appropriate investments in the proper proportions can someone hope to control the amount of investment risk without unnecessarily reducing the expected rate of return.

IDENTIFYING INDIVIDUAL GOALS

The initial step in controlling risk is to identify the goal or goals that an investment program is designed to achieve. It may seem unlikely that a rational person will invest funds when no specific motives have been identified. Investments can be made only at the expense of reducing current consumption, and few find pleasure in giving up many of life's pleasures.

The truth is that individuals all too frequently acquire investments without really defining what it is that they expect the investments to accomplish. When asked for reasons why they are investing, many individuals simply reply, "to make money." Granted, earning a return is the bottom line of any investment plan. However, it should normally be viewed as a means to an end. More clearly defined goals must be determined or chaos will result. The self-described goal "to make money" frequently leads investors to commit funds in a piecemeal manner that produces a kind of "portfolio of the damned"—a group of assets that has no coherence and accomplishes no purpose. Setting goals involves more than simply attempting to make money.

Identifying goals is crucial to establishing an intelligent investment program, because an individual's goals play a major role in determining the risks that can be tolerated and, hence, the kinds of investment assets that should be acquired. For example, if achieving a particular goal is deemed to be absolutely crucial, then certain restrictions apply to the investments that are to be acquired in pursuit of the goal. The same limitations may be less important or even irrelevant when the achievement of a goal is desirable but not really critical.

Examples of investment goals include accumulating funds for sending children to college, establishing a retirement fund to supplement social security and perhaps an employer's retirement plan, and putting aside sufficient funds to take an extensive and expensive vacation. Other potential goals might include the accumulation of funds for the down payment on a home or the outright purchase of a sports car. It doesn't take a lot of thought to add more in-dividualized items to this list of goals. Perhaps a boat or swimming pool might even sneak their way onto some lists, for example.

One investment goal that should not be overlooked is an ade-quate emergency fund to tide one over a period of unexpected ex-penses caused by some unfortunate incident such as a wrecked automobile, a house fire, or a medical problem. The fund may also be needed in case an individual suffers an unexpected reduction or interruption of income.

SELECTING INVESTMENTS APPROPRIATE TO THE GOAL

Once goals have been identified, the next order of business in con-trolling investment risk is to select assets compatible with the goals. Unless investments are suitable for a portfolio designed to attain certain goals, an investor will face unnecessary risks that can or-dinarily be minimized, or, in some cases, entirely eliminated. The result is likely to be a portfolio of investments that will not achieve the desired results.

Two important considerations when selecting appropriate invest-ments are the relative importance of the identified goal and the length of time until the goal is to be attained. Understanding these two attributes will go a long way in determining the types of invest-ments most appropriate in meeting the goal.

Relative Importance of a Goal

The more important a goal is considered to be, the less room there is for assets that subject the investor to uncertain returns. In other words, the more important the goal, the less risk that should be inherent in the investments acquired to achieve the goal. For ex-ample, a goal of providing an adequate retirement income for someone who is near retirement age is a very important goal for nearly anyone. Thus, relatively little risk can be tolerated, even though this means that the expected returns are limited. On the other hand, a goal that is considered to be significantly less impor-tant, say the purchase of a boat for occasional weekend use or a beautiful 1957 Chevrolet, presents an instance in which an individual can tolerate investments with greater risks and higher expected returns.

A potential loss of principal is the risk to be minimized when the achievement of an investment goal is considered to be very important. As a result, an individual should select investment alternatives that minimize both financial and business risk. It would not be good policy to invest in speculative stocks, even those paying relatively high dividends, in order to finance a retirement, for example.

Minimizing risks that can deplete principal doesn't mean that there is absolutely no room for uncertainty and that all funds should be committed to Treasury securities. It does mean that the investor should favor high-grade securities over speculative stocks.

The Length of Time for a Goal to Be Achieved

The length of time between when a goal is identified and when the required funds will be needed is a significant factor in determining the risks that can be tolerated and, consequently, the types of assets that should be acquired. As a rule, a longer period of time before funds are needed means that uncertainties caused by interest-rate risk, reinvestment risk, market risk, and liquidity risk are generally of reduced importance. The uncertain returns caused by these risks tend to be cyclical, and a long holding period minimizes the possibility that an individual will have to liquidate an asset during a down phase in a cycle.

Uncertain returns caused by purchasing-power risk, financial risk, and business risk are the overriding concerns for investors looking at long-term goals. The almost complete loss of principal from business and financial collapse can cause real grief for an investor attempting to attain some long-term objective. Even if principal remains intact in dollar terms, unexpectedly high inflation can produce severe losses in purchasing power over a long period, so that the real value of an investor's assets can be devastated.

An investor with long-term goals does have some breathing room from the uncertainties produced by these risks, however. A goal to be achieved many years in the future allows time to recover from a mistake. For example, an investor with a goal to be achieved in 20 years can suffer significant losses in the first several years and still have another 15 to 17 years to bounce back. Such an unpleasant event will require an increase in annual savings in subsequent years, but at least recovery is still possible. Because of the recovery time for long-term goals, an investor can generally choose investments with higher risks and higher expected returns than if the goals are short-term.

As the time changes until a goal is to be achieved, an investor will need to revise the rankings of the various risks. Generally, the revision occurs because of a reduction in time as the date on which a goal is to be achieved moves closer. Liquidity risk provides a good example of an uncertainty that changes in importance as an investor's time horizon is shortened. Liquidity risk is of very little concern over a longer term but has great significance when funds will be needed in a few months or even a few years. Likewise, uncertainties caused by market movements and interest-rate changes become very important to someone who expects to liquidate all or a portion of an investment in a relatively short time. The changing importance of various risks caused by the timing changes of investment goals means that investors must constantly monitor and occasionally alter investment positions over time, even though the goal itself remains unchanged.

ASSET ALLOCATION

An investor must determine the relative importance that different types of assets will assume in a portfolio. It is just as important to acquire appropriate amounts of particular assets as it is to select suitable assets in the first place. Thus, after an investor has established that high-grade bonds are an appropriate investment to meet an identified goal, the next step is to determine what proportion of the investor's total portfolio should be composed of high-grade bonds.

For the majority of investors the proper blend of assets will vary as these individuals pass through different stages of their lives. Thus, a young couple with small children will not want the same combination of assets as an individual who is single. Each of these, in turn, will not select the same asset mix as a retired couple. These three family units have very different needs and equally different goals. The concerns about various uncertainties they will face from owning different assets will assume different perspectives for each unit.

Asset allocation is a macro view of selecting appropriate investments for meeting identified goals, because it represents the composite of all of the assets that have been acquired. This overall view permits an investor to monitor a single large portfolio rather than a multitude of small portfolios designed for meeting individual goals. Only when all of the assets are combined and viewed as a whole can an individual get a handle on the extent to which each of the risks is inherent in the portfolio of investments that is owned.

An individual's portfolio will normally shift toward becoming more aggressive (more risky with respect to most of the uncertainties that are faced) as the person advances toward middle age. In part, this shift represents the fact that the liquidity needs of an emergency fund have already been accommodated so that additional funds can be invested in assets that offer the prospect of capital appreciation. Thus, a single individual or a husband and wife entering their late 40's will be looking at an upcoming period of maximum earning power combined with limited responsibilities.

Diminished financial obligations stem from the likelihood that any children are already or will soon be on their own and that any remaining mortgage on a primary residence should be quite small. As a result, a family's two biggest financial burdens are likely to have been relieved, with the result that substantial amounts of after-tax income are freed to meet other goals. Specific concerns relative to each of these family units are discussed in more detail later in this chapter.

THE NEED TO PERIODICALLY REALLOCATE PORTFOLIO ASSETS

It is important for an investor to continually monitor the various categories of assets in a portfolio, so that changes in the values of individual investments do not cause a portfolio to become unbalanced. For example, if a particular investment, say an issue of common stock, increases substantially in value, this security is likely to comprise too great a portion of the portfolio's total value. Thus, an individual who has decided on an allocation mix of 30 percent common stocks, 40 percent long-term fixed-income securities, 20 percent tangible assets, and 10 percent money-market assets will find that the common stock component will make up a significantly larger proportion of the portfolio than intended. Assets must then be realigned by selling stock and using the proceeds to purchase other investments, until the portfolio composition returns to the desired proportions.

Reallocation is also required when the value of one asset category declines relative to the current market values of other owned assets. If a major bear market causes stocks to decline steeply in price, the dollar value of investments in the portfolio should be readjusted to bring common stocks back to their former level on a proportionate basis. Thus, some fixed-income securities or tangible assets may have to be liquidated to build the common stock portion of the portfolio back to its earlier percentage level.

Periodically evaluating the asset allocation of a portfolio doesn't mean that an individual should continually tinker with investments by switching funds back and forth between categories. Such an exercise might prove to be entertaining for someone with both the time and the inclination to fine-tune an investment program on a short-term basis, but it will also result in excessive fees. Only when the need for reallocation of a portfolio's assets becomes apparent by casual inspection is it advisable for funds to be moved between categories. If an investor holds a fairly hefty position in a stock that subsequently doubles in value, it becomes fairly obvious that some reallocation needs to take place. This allocation will involve the sale of a substantial portion of the stock and the reinvestment of funds in other categories of assets.

Most asset values will be continually changing, so that a portfolio's asset mix will vary among categories. If the individual changes are not too great, a proper portfolio composition is easier and less expensive to maintain by channeling new investment dollars into the underrepresented categories of investments than by liquidating assets and moving funds among the various sectors. This means that if common stocks fall in price so that the market value of this sector of the portfolio is too low, new funds should be allocated to similar assets in order to bring the sector back to its former position of relative importance.

USING DIVERSIFICATION TO REDUCE RISK

More than any other single act, selecting investment assets with differing attributes can mitigate the potential damage caused by the various risks that have been discussed. This process of diversification is certainly not an end-all, for other investment considerations are important for any individual. However, acquiring assets with varying investment characteristics is a relatively painless way to reduce risk without spending considerable time learning complicated investment theory. In most instances, an understanding of the concepts discussed earlier in this book combined with a little common sense are all that is required to assemble a portfolio of investments that has adequate diversification.

Assembling a Diversified Portfolio of Investments

Adequate diversification requires that an investor assemble disparate assets that are not all affected in the same manner or to the same extent by the different forces that influence investment returns. In the language of a statistician this means that proper diversification requires that the returns on the assets not be highly correlated.

A diversity in the characteristics of assets serves to protect an investor from having all or even most of the assets in a portfolio suffer large losses at the same time. Thus, just because interest rates suddenly rise or because the government suddenly decides to slash defense spending, an investor will not suffer financial losses so large as to devastate the value of an investment portfolio. There may still be losses, of course, but any significant losses that occur from holding certain assets will be tempered by returns from other assets that have different characteristics and are not affected to the same extent by the same forces.

Suppose unexpected inflation eats away at the real value of the interest payments and the eventual principal repayment of a bond more rapidly than investors had anticipated, so that real returns are penalized. While unexpected inflation hurts investors holding fixed-income securities, Chapter 6 pointed out that the unexpected increases in consumer prices will likely have a beneficial effect for investors holding precious metals. Thus, the effects of inflation on one type of asset can be at least partially offset by the effects of the same inflation on an entirely different type of asset. An investor who holds a diversified investment portfolio that includes both of these assets will have some protection against the uncertainty of unexpected decreases in purchasing power.

Diversification should be a consideration even when acquiring assets of a similar type, because it is important to have different characteristics within groups of assets as well as among groups of assets. For example, an individual should hold a diversified group of fixed-income securities at the same time that these securities are offset with common stocks and tangible assets. Because bonds of similar maturities and risk characteristics tend to offer virtually identical yields, there is no reason for an investor to concentrate all of a portfolio's fixed-income component on the bonds or the preferred stock of a single firm or even a single industry. In practice, diversification among different segments of the economy is even more important to controlling risk than is diversification among different firms within a given segment of the economy.

An investor should not forget to include his or her own capacity to earn income as a portfolio asset when considering diversification. Including an individual as an income-earning asset is a crucial consideration in putting together a diversified portfolio. If a significant portion of an individual's income is derived from earned income (as opposed to investment income), it is very important that acquired assets be diversified away from the field of employment. Having uncertain investment income at the same time that an individual's job is potentially in jeopardy is too much risk for anyone. Thus, someone who is employed by a financial institution should invest outside the industry, even though that is the very industry of which the individual has the greatest knowledge. The greater the relative importance of an individual's ability to earn income, the more compelling the need for acquiring investment assets unrelated to the individual's job.

Unfortunately, a large number of individuals find that adequate diversification through the purchase of singular investments is impractical because of the relatively small amount of funds that are periodically available for investing. Someone who has just started investing modest sums of money is unlikely to be able to create a diversified portfolio for many years. Even individuals who have accumulated a sizable sum through several years of investing will often be unable to diversify adequately. In any case, attempting any significant amount of diversification will require relatively large commissions because of the necessity of periodically purchasing small amounts of individual investments.

Diversification Through the Purchase of Investment Company Shares

Investment company shares offer individuals the opportunity to acquire a small interest in a diverse group of assets with a relatively small sum of money and at a minimal cost—minimal cost, that is, if prior to committing any money the investor is careful to investigate the size of an investment company's management fees (generally stated as a percentage of the total funds managed by the firm) and determine whether any sales or surrender charges (stated as a percentage of the dollar amount invested or redeemed) are involved with the purchase or sale of the firm's shares.

All investment companies have management fees, although these vary from ½ percent to 1 ½ percent of assets annually. Although sales fees are a one-time charge, they vary much more than annual management fees. As a rule, investment companies selling shares by mail have no sales fees, while firms that market their shares through salespeople charge a fee of up to 8 ½ percent of the funds invested. Fees vary significantly and sometimes tend to be hidden, so an investor should carefully check an investment company prospectus to determine the extent of a firm's fees.

Investment companies exist to satisfy virtually any need. Bond funds specialize in corporate bonds, government bonds, tax-exempt municipal bonds, municipal bonds subject to the alternative minimum tax, and bonds denominated in foreign currencies. There are stock funds that specialize in the shares of growth companies, energy companies, companies involved in precious metals, firms from a particular country or region of the world, and so forth. No matter what the industry or the region, there is an investment company that purchases only the shares of that specialized segment. There are also diversified investment companies that acquire a broad spectrum of common stocks and balanced investment companies that acquire a combination of common stocks and fixed-income securities.

The large selection of both specialized (called "sector funds") and broad-based investment companies permits the choice of a fund that provides diversification among many companies within a limited sector of the economy or among a broad array of industries. It is this diversification and resulting risk reduction offered by investment companies that many investors, especially those who are in the initial stages of an investment program, cannot attain through the purchase of individual assets.

Owning shares in investment companies, however, is not without significant risks. The values of these funds tend to move with the market, and the shares of specialized funds are often much more volatile than the overall market, although they would tend to be less volatile than individual stocks within the same group. Overall, investment company shares offer investors a degree of diversification that can seldom be attained through the purchase of individual investments.

Controlling risk using investment companies requires that an investor choose funds with goals similar to those that have been identified by the investor. Thus, an income fund may be appropriate for an investor close to retirement, while a growth stock fund is more likely to serve the needs of a young family putting aside funds for the future—for a retirement or a child's college education—for example. To hedge against the possibility of unexpected inflation, an investor may wish to select a fund that specializes in the common stocks of natural-resource companies.

An investor with a variety of investment needs may acquire the shares of several funds. A portion of an individual's funds may be placed in a money-market fund, while additional money will be in a growth-stock fund and a fixed-income fund. An individual can satisfy virtually any investment goal or any number of investment goals simultaneously by using investment companies. Placing funds with a company that manages several funds and permits transfers among funds at a nominal cost increases an investor's flexibility.

RISK CONSIDERATIONS OF THREE POPULAR INVESTMENT GOALS

Three frequently identified investment goals are the establishment of an emergency fund, the accumulation of a relatively large sum of money to be used for a one-time expenditure at some future time, and the provision for supplementary income to commence at a planned retirement date. There are other explanations of why individuals invest, of course, but these are three of the most common reasons, and they are sufficiently diverse that each one calls for a different strategy for controlling risk.

Accumulating an Emergency Fund

The highest investment priority for any individual or family unit is to establish an adequate emergency fund. Every individual needs to have access to a fund that can support emergency spending needs for such things as unexpected medical expenses, ordinary living expenditures during a short-term period of unemployment, or the replacement of assets that are unexpectedly lost. Even though each of these losses may be at least partially offset with appropriate insurance coverage, individuals will nearly always encounter unexpected monetary needs.

Because an emergency fund is designed to provide for unexpected difficulties, safety of principal, stability of value, and excellent liquidity are the prime considerations for assets that are selected for such a fund. These strict requirements eliminate the majority of investment vehicles from consideration. For example, common stocks, intermediate- and long-term bonds, preferred stocks, real estate, and gold bullion are not considered suitable investments for an emergency fund. These investment vehicles are all short of safety, stability, and liquidity.

More suitable investments would be shares of a money-market fund, money-market account deposits, U.S. Treasury bills, and short-term certificates of deposit. Although each of these alternatives offers limited earnings potential, the primary requisites for investments in an emergency fund are safety and liquidity, not high earnings potential.

The amount of assets that should be kept in an emergency fund vary, depending on the amount of an individual's income, liabilities, and the size and types of assets owned. Most knowledgeable estimates are in the range of three to six months of after-tax income, although the level depends on the portion of income that an individual spends. The lower the ratio of spending to after-tax income, the fewer months of after-tax income that need to be accumulated in an emergency fund.

The cost of maintaining an emergency fund is a function of the reduced return earned by the fund's investments compared to the expected returns that could be earned from investments not suitable for this purpose. Reduced return is only part of the consideration, however. An investor who has accumulated an adequate emergency fund can reduce some other expenses in order to offset at least a portion of the expected loss of income. For example, a sizable emergency fund can reduce the need for various kinds of insurance. An individual with an adequate emergency fund might decide to increase the size of the deductibles on most property and casualty insurance policies. Health insurance and disability income insurance are additional candidates for deductible increases.

Saving for a Major Expenditure

Everyone has a number of relatively expensive material things they would like to acquire and at least a few costly activities in which they would like to participate. Many of these material items and activities are sufficiently important that a person is willing to forego current consumption to have a chance of accumulating the funds required to eventually make the acquisition.

Some assets and activities are so expensive that a plan may be necessary in order to have a reasonable chance of accumulating the required funds. Examples of such high-cost assets and activities

abound: a college education for one or more children, a down payment on a new home, a vacation home, an extensive vacation, a
new car, an expensive boat, and so forth. For many individuals the
list seems endless.

After setting priorities for the identified goals, it is necessary to
determine the money that will be required to make a particular
acquisition and the approximate time when the goal is to be
achieved. The cost estimate must take into account the expected
cost at the time the acquisition is to take place. In other words, it is
necessary to incorporate any expected increase in the cost of the
asset or activity. Only after these tasks have been accomplished can
an individual consider the types of investments appropriate in
meeting the goal.

An earlier section of this chapter discussed the importance of
considering the time between when investments are made and
when funds are needed in determining the types of investments to
use. If the period of time is quite long, as would be the case for
funding the college education of a recently-born child, investment
vehicles such as common stocks, intermediate- or long-term bonds,
or other assets that involve relatively long holding periods are appropriate candidates for acquisition.

On the other hand, if funds will be needed relatively soon, say in
three or four years, investing in common stocks and long-term
bonds is likely to entail too much of the wrong kinds of risk. Uncertainties caused by market variations and interest-rate changes are
critical when a short holding period is planned. Depending on the
types of securities used, business risk, financial risk, and liquidity
risk could also prove to be problems.

A consideration discussed earlier in this chapter is the relative
importance of the goal. In general, the more critical a particular goal
is considered, the more that return will have to be sacrificed for
reduced risk. Suppose a husband and wife decide that providing
their only daughter with the funds for a college education is an
absolute necessity. In such a case the parents should choose investments that have very small business and financial risks. Even a
moderate possibility of losing a large portion of the principal from
an investment because of a bad business environment or because of

the inability of an issuer to meet financial obligations is not something the parents should be willing to accept.

If the funds accumulated to finance the education will not be required until many years in the future (depending on the daughter's age), investments with relatively long time horizons are most appropriate. Of course, nonmarketable investments could be used, but the low returns earned from these investments are generally too great a penalty, considering the risks that can reasonably be accepted. One of the great advantages of nonmarketable investments is that they have virtually no market risk; however, this advantage is only marginally useful in pursuing a long-term financial goal, because market cycles are not a particular concern until close to the date the investments are to be liquidated.

Investing for Retirement

Ideally, planning for retirement should begin many years prior to the date when employment is to be terminated and supplementary income will be needed. The earlier an individual begins saving to meet the needs of retirement, the less the dollar amount of money that must be set aside in each working year to ensure adequate funds will be available when they are needed.

Someone who commences a retirement program at age 32 with the expectation of working until age 67 will have 35 years to accumulate a fund that must provide supplementary income for a minimum of 15 to 20 years. With the extended time frame generally involved in accumulating a pool of funds to provide retirement income, investments chosen for the task can have relatively long time horizons and subject their owners to at least moderate amounts of most risks and substantial amounts of some risks. This flexibility in the selection of investment assets is progressively reduced as an individual approaches retirement. Thus, an individual who is five years from retirement faces a much narrower list of investment possibilities than someone who is 20 to 30 years from retirement.

One of the greatest threats facing someone establishing a retirement fund is the possibility for significant losses in purchasing power because of unexpected increases in consumer prices. With

the long time span between when funds are saved and when retirement income will be needed, a genuine chance exists that inflation
will severely deplete the real value of the accumulated funds and
the income these funds produce. What appears to be a significant
amount of money at age 30 may have relatively little purchasing
power when a person retires 35 years later.

A concern about depleted purchasing power indicates that an
investment portfolio for retirement calls for a heavy emphasis on
investment vehicles that can provide some protection against purchasing-power risk. For example, common stocks and real assets
that tend to offset inflation over long periods of time are prime
candidates for inclusion. Common stocks should include companies
that tend to show higher earnings and increased asset values following a lengthy period of inflation. Stocks of natural resource
companies such as petroleum and forest products firms should be
considered, for example.

The fluctuating values of investment assets caused by interest-
rate changes and general market fluctuations are not a great concern for investors investing for a distant retirement. Interest rates
and market movements can be expected to go through numerous
cycles during the years when assets are being accumulated for a
retirement fund. Uncertainties caused by these cycles are more important in the short run than the long run. Of course, as the time
when the funds are needed moves nearer, market risk becomes
considerably more important, so that an investor will almost surely
want to begin switching some assets several years before investments are to be tapped for funds.

Liquidity risk is only a minor concern for someone investing for a
faraway retirement. Assets such as individual issues of corporate or
municipal bonds that frequently lack liquidity in the secondary
market will likely have matured prior to the time funds are required. Other investments such as real assets and infrequently
traded common stocks will have to be sold only after a relatively
long holding period, so that the one-time price concession that may
have to be offered by the seller will result in only a small reduction
in the overall yield. On the other hand, investments like money-
market funds, which subject their owners to no liquidity risk, are of

no particular advantage to someone investing for a retirement many years in the future.

Even financial risk and business risk, two uncertainties that stem from reductions in principal as well as in the payment of current income, can be tolerated to a limited extent by most investors putting aside funds for retirement. The key is to reduce the degree of both of these risks as retirement grows nearer and to accept the risks in no more than moderate amounts at any time.

One reason for accepting at least a moderate amount of both financial risk and business risk is to expand the variety of assets that can be acquired. This increased flexibility will permit an individual to include assets that will protect against some other risks at the same time that the overall portfolio should produce a higher expected rate of return. With a goal that does not have to be achieved for many years, any losses occasioned by either business or financial risk can be compensated for in succeeding years. This can occur, of course, only if the losses are not severe and do not occur close to the date that funds are needed. In other words, a limited amount of these risks is okay, but a substantial amount is a no-no.

A FINAL STATEMENT ON CONTROLLING RISK

The keys to controlling risk are to understand why investments are being made, to select investments compatible with goals, and to acquire a diversified portfolio of assets. It is senseless to concentrate funds in a single investment, industry, or type of investment. Diversification costs little and produces much. No matter how sure an investment may seem, there is always the chance that something can go wrong and funds can be lost. Effective diversification is the single most effective way to ensure that the losses are limited.

SELF-HELP QUESTIONS

1. What goals have you set for yourself or your family? What is the final dollar cost of each of these goals? Have you factored inflation into your cost estimate?

2. How much income do you feel will be necessary to support your retirement? How much of this will you have to provide from sources other than social security and a pension from your employer? What size retirement fund will you have to accumulate to provide this extra income?

3. To what extent is your own investment portfolio diversified? Do you feel that you have made an attempt to diversify or has your portfolio accumulated in more of a random manner? List one or more examples of rational diversification you have undertaken.

4. At your current age, what risks are you most concerned about? What types of investments minimize these risks? How much protection do the investments in your current portfolio offer against these risks?

5. How much do you feel is adequate for your own emergency fund? How much have you allocated to such a fund? How liquid are the assets in your emergency fund?

6. In terms of your own needs, what attributes of an investment company are most important? How would you locate a fund with the characteristics you are seeking? What are the advantages and disadvantages of purchasing securities indirectly through investment company shares?

7. In what ways do you see the mix of your investment portfolio shifting over the next decade? How do you plan to go about making this shift? Can you think of any circumstances that would cause you to change your current asset mix?

Appendix A

APPENDIX A

DURATION: A MEASURE OF BOND PRICE VOLATILITY

Chapter 4 pointed out that the price volatility of a fixed-income security varies directly with the maturity length and indirectly with the coupon size. Thus, a bond with a long maturity can be expected to fall substantially in price whenever market interest rates increase. The price decline is partially offset, however, if the bond has a relatively high coupon that permits the investor to recover a large portion of the cash flows from owning the bond prior to the final maturity date. On the other hand, a bond with a long maturity and a relatively low coupon will produce an especially large decline in price. If market rates of interest decline, a bond with a low coupon and a long maturity will produce a substantial gain in price.

Because both the maturity length and coupon size are important in determining a bond's price volatility, a measure incorporating both of these features is preferable to the normal procedure in which only maturity is considered. Fortunately, duration is a measure that takes into account both the timing and size of coupon payments as well as the recovery of principal.

Duration is defined as the weighted average time to a full recovery of principal and interest payments. It is an alternate way—

most financial advisors would say a superior way—of examining
the life of a fixed-income security. Essentially, duration is the number of years it takes to recover the present value of all future cash
payments. Duration is calculated as:

$$D = \frac{\displaystyle\sum_{t=1}^{n} \frac{C_t\,(t)}{(1+i)^t}}{\displaystyle\sum_{t=1}^{n} \frac{C_t}{(1+i)^t}}$$

where:
t = the time period when the payment occurs
C_t = the payment in period t
i = the current market return on the security

Both the concept of duration and the above formula are best explained by a comparison of two bonds of equal maturity but different coupons. Exhibit A–1 illustrates the calculation of duration
for two bonds, each with a maturity of five years. Bond A has a
4-percent coupon and Bond B has an 8-percent coupon. Assuming a
current market rate of interest of 8 percent, Bond A will sell at a
discount, in this case $845.92, while Bond B will sell at par, because
its coupon is equal to the current market rate of interest.

Duration is calculated by finding the present value of each cash
flow (column 4) and dividing the answer by the current market
price of the bond in order to compute the cash flow's present value
in terms of the percentage it represents of the bond's market price
(column 5). This percentage is then multiplied by the period in
which the cash will be received (column 1) to calculate the factors
that are summed to find the bond's duration (column 6).

Exhibit A–1 illustrates that the higher coupon 8-percent bond has
a lower duration of 4.3125 years as opposed to 4.5935 years for the
4-percent coupon bond. This smaller duration is to be expected,
because the 8-percent coupon bond returns a greater proportion of
its cash from the earlier interest payments. Only when a bond
makes no periodic interest payments (e.g., a zero-coupon bond) is
the duration equal to the number of years to maturity. For any

Exhibit A-1
Computation of Duration

Bond A — 4% coupon with 5-year maturity

1 Year	2 Cash Flow	3 PV @ 8%	4 PV of Flow	5 PV as % of Price	6 1 × 5
1	$ 40	.9259	$ 37.04	.0438	.0438
2	40	.8573	34.29	.0405	.0810
3	40	.7938	31.75	.0375	.1125
4	40	.7350	29.40	.0348	.1392
5	1,040	.6806	713.44	.8434	4.2170
			$845.92		4.5935

Bond B — 8% coupon with 5-year maturity

1 Year	2 Cash Flow	3 PV @ 8%	4 PV of Flow	5 PV as % of Price	6 1 × 5
1	$ 80	.9259	$ 74.07	.0741	.0741
2	80	.8573	68.59	.0686	.1372
3	80	.7938	63.50	.0635	.1905
4	80	.7350	58.80	.0588	.2352
5	80	.6806	735.05	.7351	3.6755
	1,080		$1,000.00		4.3125

bond with a coupon greater than zero, the duration is shorter than the time to maturity.

From an investor's point of view duration is a valuable tool, because it indicates the percentage change in a bond's price in response to a given change in yield. For example, if a bond has a duration of 12 years and yields change by 2 percent, the bond will change in price by approximately 24 percent (12 times 2). Thus, duration provides a much better measure of a bond's price volatility than does maturity length alone.

Duration also provides guidance on the specific coupon and maturity of a bond to purchase in order to meet a goal on a specific date. This is true because duration incorporates both potential price changes and changes in the rate at which cash flows can be reinvested. Thus, an investor who has a specific goal to accomplish in 10 years has a better idea of what a bond will accomplish if the bond has a duration of 10 years than if the bond has a maturity of 10 years.

Appendix B

BOND RATINGS

A bond rating is a grading of a fixed-income security on the basis of a professional analysis by independent firms. The two largest and best-known agencies are Standard & Poor's and Moody's. Two additional rating agencies are Fitch Investors Service and Duff and Phelps. These firms rate the debt securities of corporations, cities, states, and even some federal agencies and make these ratings available to both individual and institutional investors.

Rating agencies do a fundamental analysis of issuers and individual issues, thus saving investors from performing this task themselves. Individual investors rely heavily on published ratings, so that the rating of a particular issue has a major impact on the interest rate that must be paid in order to sell the debt issue. Receiving a higher rating on an debt issue can save an organization millions of dollars in interest expense over the life of the issue. New issues of bonds are relatively difficult to market without a rating so that organizations wishing to issue debt securities are willing to pay the rating agencies to grade their debt and make the grading public. While this payment on the part of the organizations seeking a rating for their debt issues may seem to pose a conflict of interest, the rating agencies can only survive by preserving a reputation of high ethical standards and accurate evaluations.

Bond analysis is considerably different from the analysis of common stocks. A financially strong firm may have debt that is very highly rated at the same time that its common stock is considered less than desirable. A major reason for this dissimilarity is the fact that growth in revenues and income drives common stocks, while bond quality centers more around the ability of an issuer to service an issue of debt over its lifetime. The rating agencies will alter the rating of an issue after the issue has been sold if the ability of the issuer to service this debt changes significantly. Thus, bonds may be downgraded or upgraded by the agencies following events such as takeovers, major acquisitions, or a string of earnings declines.

Exhibit B–1 shows the various rating categories of the two major rating agencies. The grades and categories are virtually identical for both firms, and individual issues are generally rated the same by both organizations. In some cases an issue may have a split rating, meaning that the two firms view an issue differently. For example, Standard & Poor's may assign a rating of AA while Moody's grades the same issue as an A. In other instances an issue may be rated by only a single agency.

Standard and Poor's uses plus (+) and minus (–) to indicate relative differences within a rating category while Moody's uses the numbers 1, 2, and 3 for the same purpose. For example, ratings of BBB+ and Baa1 both indicate issues that are judged to be at the high end of this investment-grade category. A rating of at least BBB (S&P) or Baa (Moody's) is necessary for an issue to be considered as investment grade. Issues with ratings below this level are frequently referred to as junk bonds, although some individuals restrict this designation to bonds rated B and below. Bonds with ratings of B and below offer relatively high yields but carry significant risks for investors.

Although the quality of an issuer is very important in determining a rating, it is the issue rather than the issuer that is assigned a rating. Thus, it is possible for a single issuer to have different issues of outstanding debt with different ratings. Issues of the same organization can vary according to maturity, collateral, and the hierarchy of an issue in the debt structure of the issuer. Debentures (unsecured debt) tend to be rated lower and carry a higher rate of interest than secured bonds issued by the same firm.

Exhibit B–1
Bond Ratings

Moody's	S&P	
Aaa	AAA	High-grade with extremely strong capacity to pay principal and interest.
Aa	AA	High-grade by all standards but with slightly lower margins of protection than AAA.
A	A	Medium-grade with favorable investment attributes but with some susceptibility to adverse economic changes.
Baa	BBB	Medium-grade with adequate capacity to pay interest and principal but possibly lacking certain protection against adverse economic conditions.
Ba	BB	Speculative with moderate protection of principal and interest in an unstable economy.
B	B	Speculative and lacking desirable characteristics of investment bonds. Small assurance of principal and interest.
Caa	CCC	Issue in default or in danger of default.
Ca	CC	Highly speculative and in default or with other market shortcomings.
C		Extremely poor investment quality.
	C	Income bonds paying no interest.
D		In default with interest or principal in arrears.

Appendix C

BETA: A MEASURE OF SYSTEMATIC RISK

The uncertainty surrounding the rate of return from an investment is caused both by forces that affect all investments and by forces unique to a particular investment. The unique portion of the risk is called "unsystematic risk" and includes events such as labor strife, natural calamities, and unfavorable regulatory judgments. Because unsystematic risk is unique to individual investments, it is possible for an investor to minimize its effects by acquiring a diversified portfolio. A portfolio of at least eight diversified investments will reduce unsystematic risk to a very low level. Not surprisingly, unsystematic risk is frequently called "diversifiable risk."

Systematic risk is the result of forces that affect all investments. Because systematic risk is universal, it also goes under the name "nondiversifiable risk" and includes such events as inflation and interest-rate movements. Although systematic risk is applicable to all investments, it does not occur to each to the same degree. Some investments have a high degree of nondiversifiable risk, while other investments have relatively low nondiversifiable risk.

Beta is a measure of systematic risk, in that it shows how the return on a security can be expected to respond to market forces. The greater the response of an investment to the market, the greater the nondiversifiable risk and the greater the beta. When an investment's return responds weakly to market forces the investment has a low beta. Because a beta of one is the systematic risk of the market and the average among all investments, a beta of more than one indicates greater-than-average nondiversifiable risk.

Exhibit C–1 shows the method for determining the beta of a single investment based on historical returns from both the investment and the market. The returns from the asset are measured vertically, while historical returns on the market are measured along the horizontal axis. Point A is the result of one period, when the investment returned 9 percent and the market returned 7 percent. Point B represents the result of a second period, when the investment returned 12 percent to the market's 8 percent. Other points on the graph are derived from the combinations of the two returns for other periods.

After a sufficient number of data points are plotted on the graph, a straight line is fitted to the data in such a way that the line minimizes the squared distances between all of the points and the line. The slope of the line shows the responsiveness of the investment's return to the market's return and is the investment's beta. The more responsive the investment's returns are to the returns from the market, the steeper the slope of the line and the higher the investment's beta.

An investment with a high beta is not necessarily undesirable, because the investment should have a higher expected return than an investment with a low beta. The question is whether the individual investor is willing to pay the price of the greater risk in order to earn a higher expected return. The actual return on a high beta stock may well be significantly higher or significantly lower than the expected return over a given time. That, of course, is the risk. On the other hand, a low beta stock is more likely to produce a return close to its expected return.

The beta for a portfolio of investments is equal to the weighted values of the betas of individual investments within the portfolio. Thus, the greater the importance of a particular investment to a portfolio, the greater the influence of that investment's beta on the portfolio beta. If a portfolio contains three investments with betas of .6, .8, and 1.2 in proportions of 20 percent, 50 percent, and 30 per-

Exhibit C-1
Derivation of Beta

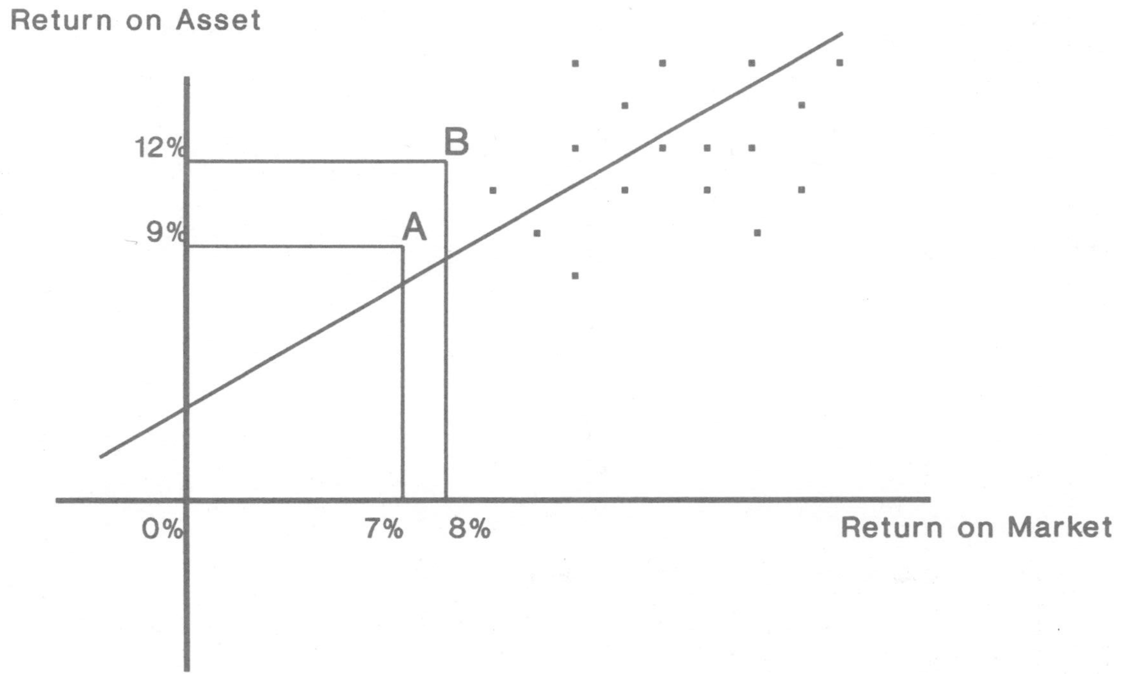

Return on Asset

12%

9%

B

A

0%   7%   8%

Return on Market

cent, respectively, the portfolio beta is calculated as $(.2 \times .6) + (.5 \times .8) + (.3 \times 1.2) = .88$.

Investment	Proportion in Portfolio		Investment Beta		Weighted Beta
A	.20	×	.6	=	.12
B	.50	×	.8	=	.40
C	.30	×	1.2	=	.36
Portfolio	1.00				.88

Appendix D

ANSWERS TO
END-OF-CHAPTER
SELF-HELP QUESTIONS

CHAPTER 1

1. Because Investment B has such a large range of possible returns and the same expected return as Investment A, a risk-averse investor would tend to prefer the assured return of Investment A. Even though Investment B has a one-year shorter maturity, the slightly earlier return of principal would not offset the greater risk of the uncertain returns.

   The increased range of possible outcomes would make Investment B even less desirable for a risk-averse investor so that the preference for Investment A should remain unchanged.

   An important consideration for both investments is the timing of the cash flows. For example, Investment A may promise a 7 percent annual return but make a single payment combining principal and all accrued interest at the end of year 5.

2.   The risk-free return is generally considered to be the return that is available on Treasury bills. Treasury bills are auctioned each Monday with the auction results carried in the Tuesday editions of most major newspapers. Inflation figures are announced monthly although inflationary expectations relative to futures rates may be different from the prevailing rate.

3.   The capacity to assume risk is greater for someone who is young, wealthy, and has few financial reponsibilities. Because these characteristics are unique for different investors, the capacity to assume risk must be evaluated on an individual basis.

4.   It is frequently worthwhile to view risk on a relative basis in order to evaluate one's own capacity to withstand financial reverses. In comparing themselves with others, individuals are often able to distinguish considerations that would tend to be overlooked. Things to be considered might include number and age of dependents, spending patterns, size and security of income, and accumulated wealth.

5.   Individuals will sometimes acquire investments without really considering their ability to assume risk. Spending time to determine how one feels about risk is a necessary part of choosing investment vehicles that conform to the needs and goals of an individual investor. One way to improve the process is to evaluate the capacity of others to assume investment risk.

6.   The answer to this question is really the bottom line to this book. That is, do the investments that you already own fit the risk profile that you have identified? For many investors the answer is no because they acquire investments without considering either their own capacity to assume risk or how the risk characteristics of a new investment vehicle affect the overall risk of their existing portfolio of investments.

     If an investor determines that existing investments are either too risky or not sufficiently risky, it is generally less expensive to adjust a portfolio's riskiness through new acquisitions rather than through a wholesale turnover of existing assets.

CHAPTER 2

1. Even though world-class economists have a relatively poor track record in forecasting inflation over anything other than relatively short periods of time, it is impossible for an individual to intelligently evaluate investment vehicles without incorporating some estimate for future inflation. This may consist of nothing other than estimating the future rate of inflation from the existing inflation rate although this can often prove to be very inaccurate.

2. Investments that pay fixed returns offer little protection against inflation that turns out to be significantly larger than expected. Other investments, especially those of a tangible nature such as real estate and collectibles, offer significant protection against unexpectedly large inflation but they may be negatively affected by inflation that is lower than expected.

    Because changes in inflationary expectations are so difficult to accurately forecast, an investor should acquire a diversified portfolio of investments that hedges against changes in inflationary expectations.

3. Different occupations are affected differently by changes in the inflation rate. Some individuals may actually find that their economic position improves because of inflation while others are negatively affected. Individuals who feel that their real earned income would be adversely affected by an upsurge of inflation should consider devoting a larger proportion of their investment portfolio to assets that offer protection from rising consumer prices.

4. Increased inflationary expectations tend to increase the returns that investors demand from an investment. Thus, if the return provided by an investment is not expected to change during a period when inflationary expectations in-

crease, the investment must fall in price in order to provide new investors with a higher return. On the other hand, an investment that provides returns that are directly influenced by changing inflation is less likely to have its market price altered as a result of changes in inflationary expectations. Ownership positions in natural resource companies are an example of this latter category.

5. The Federal Reserve influences interest rates through control of the money supply. This tool is so powerful that interest rates change merely because of speculation about actions the Fed will take.

    Although Federal Reserve members are appointed for long terms, there is constant pressure from elected officials to lower interest rates in order to stimulate economic activity and lower unemployment. In the long run such a policy is likely to stimulate price inflation.

6. In general, the market values of long-term investments such as common stocks, bonds with long maturities, and real estate will be adversely affected by rising interest rates. The market values of short-term investments such as money-market funds, savings accounts, and short-term certificates of deposit are not affected by rising interest rates.

    Investors expecting higher interest rates should switch funds from long-term investments to investments with short maturities. Unfortunately, interest-rate changes are very difficult to forecast.

7. When securities will soon be redeemed at face value there is little movement in the market value of the securities regardless of any changes in market interest rates. A portfolio heavily weighted with nonmarketable investments and short-term securities will experience little variations in market values regardless of what happens to market rates of interest. Portfolios with substantial amounts of common stocks and long-term debt will vary significantly in value from changes in interest rates.

CHAPTER 3

1. Investors sometimes acquire risky investments during periods of economic prosperity in order to reach for higher rates of return. Unfortunately, the market values of these investments may be severely affected by an economic downturn. Examples of investments that are likely to be severely impacted by deteriorating economic conditions include speculative common stocks and low-rated debt securities.

2. Checking the grade assigned to a debt security by a bond-rating agency is a good method of determining the ability of the issuer to service the debt in a deteriorating economic environment. As a rule, bonds rated lower than BBB are considered less than investment grade. Investors in common stocks might investigate an issuer's stability of income during prior years and the proportion of income paid as dividends.

    The proportion of total income provided by investments is a very important consideration in selecting investments for a portfolio. In general, the greater the relative importance of investment income to total income, the more conservative the investments that should be purchased.

3. The proportion of assets financed by debt can be determined from investigating the assets and liabilities of a firm's balance sheet. A greater proportion of debt generally indicates greater risk from owning securities issued by the firm. Investors should be able and willing to suffer the potential losses that may occur if they select investments with reduced credit ratings.

4. A high proportion of funds devoted to savings accounts, money-market funds, Treasury bills, and short-term certificates of deposit will result in substantial reductions of income when interest rates decline. On the other hand, ownership of long-term assets generally protects income levels for long periods of time.

5. One of the prime considerations in selecting appropriate investments is to determine the importance of a steady stream of income. For the majority of individuals planning a nearby retirement, a predictable stream of income is very important.

6. Assets of a highly liquid nature are generally not subject to market risk. For example, savings accounts and money-market funds have no market risk. At the opposite extreme, speculative common stocks and tangible assets subject their owners to substantial amounts of market risk. In general, investors must be willing to sacrifice return in order to reduce market risk.

7. Assets such as real estate, annuities, ownership in a closely held company, and many issues of stocks and bonds frequently lack liquidity so that an investor who is forced to sell on short notice may have to accept a severe price penalty compared to what could be obtained from a sale when time was of less importance. Assets with limited liquidity should be combined with assets that are more liquid in case funds have to be raised in a hurry.

CHAPTER 4

1. A portfolio heavily weighted toward long-term, fixed-income securities is subject to substantial variations in market values when interest rates change. The portfolio is also subject to having the real purchasing power of both income and principal eaten away by rising consumer prices. Such a portfolio is more appropriate to someone requiring current investment income in order to meet living expenses. Investors should constantly monitor the balance of their investment portfolio and reevaluate their need for current investment income.

2. An investment paying 9 percent during a period of 6-percent inflation is providing a real return of only 3 percent annually. Of course, it is necessary to account for changing market

values as well as current income in computing the return on an investment.

3. The need for current income, current asset holdings, a comparison between the returns on fixed-income securities and other investment vehicles, and inflationary expectations are all factors to consider when purchasing fixed-income securities. Because these factors are constantly changing, an investor must evaluate investments in terms of the current environment rather than the climate that existed when the assets were acquired.

4. Fixed-income assets have varying degrees of liquidity. For example, some bonds are rarely traded so that investors may have to accept reduced prices if it is necessary to sell the bonds in a short period of time. At the same time, other long-term bonds are actively traded on a daily basis and are easy to dispose of at near the current market price. If an investor has adequate liquidity and anticipates no need to liquidate investments prior to maturity it may be wise to acquire fixed-income securities with reduced liquidity because these investments tend to provide a slightly higher return.

5. This very dilemma faced savers during the early 1980s. The appropriate length of a certificate of deposit depends upon a number of factors including when the funds will be needed and the investor's expectations relative to future changes in interest rates. If the investment horizon is five years and the investor expects rates to fall, it would be wise to accept the slightly reduced return on the five-year certificate in order to lock in the rate for five years.

   Penalties for early withdrawal of certificates of deposit vary by institution. Investors interested in certificates of deposit should always check on an institution's penalties for early redemption prior to purchasing a CD.

6. This point was addressed earlier but it is so important that it is worth going over one more time. Purchasing bonds with other than investment-grade ratings subjects an investor to

substantial risk of loss of income in the event of a severe economic downturn. The higher yields available on low-grade securities should always be balanced against this risk.

7.   Choosing between these two investments depends upon a variety of considerations including an investor's current investments, financial obligations, and current income. An individual's psychological ability to acquire risky investments and still sleep at night is another important consideration. Thus, the appropriate answer is different for different individuals.

8.   Although investors frequently choose short-term securities when these assets provide a higher current yield, such a course of action can be a mistake. The reason is that when short-term securities yield more than long-term securities, the investment community is generally anticipating a decline in interest rates. Thus, the owner of the short-term security may have to reinvest the funds at a reduced rate of return.

CHAPTER 5

1.   A common problem among investors is to have too great a concentration in either common stocks or in fixed-income securities. The correct proportion of common stock investments depends upon a number of factors that are unique to each individual investor.

   As a rule, investors might wish to reduce the proportion of their portfolio that is dedicated to common stocks as they approach retirement. It is also important to continually review a portfolio's composition because market values of individual investments are constantly changing.

2.   Growth stocks are generally more appropriate for young and middle-age individuals while income stocks are sought by individuals nearing retirement or needing current income. Growth stocks tend to be more risky at the same time that they offer greater opportunity for capital appreciation. In ad-

dition, growth stocks have the tax advantage of deferring taxes on appreciation until gains are realized through a sale.

3. Because common stocks have a claim on a firm's earnings and assets, both of which should generally increase during periods of inflation, these securities are generally considered a hedge against rising consumer prices. After all, it is the prices being charged by these businesses that are rising.

Not all companies are able to pass through higher costs to customers. Likewise, the market values of all assets are not affected to the same degree by inflation. The common stocks of companies that are unable to pass along higher labor or capital costs to consumers offer less protection against unexpected inflation.

4. Investors should strongly consider the types of risks that they consider most important when they select common stocks. For example, someone concerned about liquidity risk should stick with actively traded common stocks that can be resold without difficulty. Likewise, an investor concerned about the erosion of purchasing power because of inflation should acquire common stocks of natural resource companies or firms with a monopoly position that are able to pass through price increases to consumers. The bottom line is that not all common stocks are created equal so that an investor must be choosy in selecting securities that are appropriate for his or her own situation.

5. One common problem that has plagued individual investors throughout history is that they often make purchases during the late stages of a bull market. The inevitable downturn then results in these individuals engaging in panic selling. Many investment advisors suggest that individual investors would be best served by employing a policy of consistently investing through both bull markets and bear markets in the belief that over the long run a diversified portfolio of common stocks will produce attractive returns. If even the professionals have difficulty outguessing market movements it may be best for individual investors not to try.

6. Individual investments should always be evaluated in terms of how they will affect an investor's overall portfolio. A common stock may be much less risky when evaluated in terms of how it affects an existing portfolio than when it is considered in isolation. For example, an investor with a portfolio that is heavily concentrated in fixed-income assets may actually reduce investment risk by acquiring shares of common stocks.

7. In most respects common stocks are more risky than fixed-income securities because common stockholders have claim only to what remains after obligations to fixed-income investors have been satisfied. However, in some respects common stocks are actually less risky. For example, in terms of protection against unanticipated inflation, common stocks tend to offer significantly more protection than do fixed-income securities. Likewise, many common stocks are more actively traded than fixed-income securities so that the stocks can be sold without making major price concessions.

8. Convertible bonds are a cross between common stock and straight debt securities of the same firm. Because the issuer is legally obligated to make interest payments and principal repayments on convertible debt, convertibles offer more security of income than do shares of common stock. On the down side, during periods of rising stock prices, convertibles will generally appreciate proportionately less than the common stocks into which they are convertible. In short, convertible bonds are a compromise between shares of common stock and long-term debt of a given company.

CHAPTER 6

1. Investors should periodically track the market values of tangible assets that are owned. One reason to do so is for insurance purposes. More appropriate to the topic at hand, an investor should consider the amount of tangible assets that are owned when making decisions as to what types of investment assets to add to a portfolio.

2. Tangible assets are particularly effective in protecting against purchasing-power risk. Assets such as real estate, precious metals, and selected collectibles tend to perform very well during periods of inflation. Most tangible assets also offer protection against reinvestment risk since there are frequently no cash payments to reinvest. One the other hand, tangible investments often subject investors to large amounts of liquidity risk because these assets must frequently be sold at substantial discounts from market value in the event of a forced sale.

3. Tangible assets tend to be best suited to young and middle-age investors who have extended investment horizons. Individuals who are currently retired or are approaching retirement are often best served by owning investments that provide a higher current income than tangible assets generally produce.

4. Transaction costs are particularly important to an investor who has a relatively short investment horizon. Trying to make a profit when the bid price is 50 to 60 percent of the ask price requires a patient investor. Thus, investing in diamonds, stamps, coins, and other collectibles often entails a long holding period before an individual can cover even the transaction costs. Transaction costs are generally proportionately less for larger investments because dealers wish to make a minimum dollar profit per trade.

5. An investor without any tangible assets is particularly subject to purchasing-power risk because tangible assets tend to provide more protection against unexpected inflation than do the majority of financial assets. On the other hand, if inflationary expectations decline as they did during the 1980's, financial assets can be expected to outperform tangible assets. Also, investors who concentrate funds in tangible assets may well find that their portfolio becomes so illiquid that they can't take advantage of other investment opportunities that become available. As a rule, the proportion of tangible assets in an individual's portfolio should decline as the individual approachs retirement.

6.   It is frequently difficult to determine even an approximate market value for tangible assets. In many cases, even slight physical differences in assets of a similar nature can produce vastly different market values. In other cases, assets are so seldom traded that no recent market value is available. Despite these difficulties, it is important that an individual attempt to keep track of the values of tangible assets that are owned.

CHAPTER 7

1.   Nonmarketable assets are generally low-risk investment vehicles that are sought by investors who are willing to sacrifice return in order to protect principal and income. It is possible to go overboard and suffer substantial income loss from devoting too large a portion of an investment portfolio to nonmarketable investments.

2.   Yields on certificates of deposit frequently change more slowly than yields on Treasury bills so that investors should compare the returns on both investments before committing funds to either vehicle. Essentially, both of these investments are riskless so that they are comparable.

3.   There are no longer stipulated rates of interest that banks, savings and loans, and credit unions are permitted to pay on certificates of deposit. Thus, financial institions tend to pay interest rates that are required in order to attract funds in their particular location. This frequently leads to variations in the rates that are paid in different areas of the country. In addition, savers sometimes have substantial inertia in moving funds from one institution to another so that individual institutions can sometimes get away with paying below-market rates. In addition, some institutions react more slowly to changing economic conditions than do other institutions. Thus, it is important for individual investors to shop among various financial institutions before investing funds in certificates of deposit.

4. U.S. savings bonds offer certain tax advantages over certificates of deposit. Interest received from a savings bond is not taxable by state and local governments and even federal income taxes may be deferred until the year the bond is redeemed. Because the rate of interest paid on savings bonds is now variable, investors with these instruments will see their return increase if there is an increase in market rates of interest during the period the bond is owned. On the other hand, if market rates of interest decline, an investor holding a U.S. savings bond will experience a reduced return. Thus, savings bonds subject investors to more reinvestment risk than do long-term certificates of deposit.

5. Nonmarketable financial assets can generally be liquidated at face value without penalty or with only a small penalty. Thus, nonmarketable assets have no liquidity risk, market risk, or interest-rate risk. In addition, because many of these assets are insured by a government agency or guaranteed by the U.S. government, there is virtually no business risk or financial risk. Overall, nonmarketable financial assets provide investors with highly liquid, virtually risk-free investments that have a place in most individual's portfolios.

CHAPTER 8

1. Establishing goals and determining the amounts of funds required to meet the identified goals is one of the first items of business in establishing an intelligent investment program. Unfortunately, it is a task that is conveniently overlooked by many individuals.

2. The required income for a comfortable retirement depends upon a number of variables including a family's living standard and the cost of maintaining that standard at a specified time in the future. In other words, it is very important to consider inflation prior to and during retirement when estimating retirement living expenses. It is also important to understand that expense patterns will change at

retirement. For example, recreational expenses may increase at the same time that expenditures for clothing and transportation may decline substantially.

The size of a fund designated for providing retirement income depends upon the amount of annual expenses that will be required, the length of time they will be required, and the return that can be earned on the retirement fund. Individuals must also consider any income that will flow from social security and an employer's pension plan. Both of these items should be subtracted from estimated annual expenses in calculating the amount of funds that will have to be accumulated.

3. Diversification reduces the overall risk that an investor faces. Accumulating a portfolio of diversified assets means that one particular event such as a bankruptcy, inflation, or an extended bear market in stocks will not devastate an entire portfolio. Unfortunately, individuals frequently choose new investments without considering the risk characteristics of the investment assets that are already owned.

4. The importance of individual risks are different for investors of different ages. For example, an individual at or nearing retirement should make every effort to avoid loss of principal by choosing assets that minimize both business risk and financial risk. Younger investors can accept some of these risks in an attempt to earn the higher expected returns that accompany more risky investments. Retired individuals who rely on investment income to provide most of their living expenses should also spread out the maturities of their investments in order to reduce reinvestment risk.

5. Financial advisors recommend that individuals keep liquid assets equal to at least 6 months after-tax income in order to meet financial emergencies. It is important to use highly liquid assets such as money-market funds, money-market accounts at financial insitutions, or savings accounts to meet this need because the funds are often needed without delay. Having to borrow to meet emergency expenses is very ex-

pensive. Not only is the interest rate generally high but most interest is no longer deductible for federal tax purposes.

6.   There is such a diversity of investment companies that it is possible for an individual to find one or more firms that will meet virtually any individual investment goal. As a rule, the goals of an investment company should be the same as the goals of an individual investor. Thus, if an individual considers current income to be important, an investment company with a goal of maximizing current income is a good candidate for selection. Investment companies provide investors with the opportunity to diversify even a small amount of money, something that is impossible if it is necessary to acquire individual investment vehicles. The disadvantage of owning investment company shares is that these firms charge a fee.

7.   As an individual's investment goals change there should be a corresponding shift in the assets that are used to meet those goals. An investor may shift the mix of a portfolio from one that is primarily designed to provide capital appreciation to one that provides current income. Likewise, an investor increasingly concerned about inflation may wish to replace assets producing current income with natural resource stocks or some form of ownership in precious metals.

It is generally less expensive to shift the composition of a portfolio through the addition of new assets rather than through the swap of assets that are already owned.

ABOUT THE AUTHOR

David L. Scott is Professor of Accounting and Finance at Valdosta State College, Valdosta, Georgia, where he teaches courses in financial management, investments, and personal finance. Professor Scott was born in Rushville, Indiana, and earned degrees from Purdue University, Florida State University, and received his Ph.D. from the University of Arkansas at Fayetteville.

Dr. Scott has authored over a dozen books in addition to numerous articles for professional journals. His most recent book prior to *Identifying and Controlling Investment Risk* was *Wall Street Words*, published by Houghton Mifflin Company. He is also the co-author of two best-selling guides to the areas operated by the National Park Service. He and his wife, Kay, spend their summers traveling around the United States and Canada in their Volkswagen Campmobile.